CRIMINAL JUSTICE, LAW ENFORCEMENT AND CORRECTIONS SERIES

REVISITING THE SOCIAL CONTRACT: COMMUNITY JUSTICE AND PUBLIC SAFETY

CRIMINAL JUSTICE, LAW ENFORCEMENT AND CORRECTIONS SERIES

Homicide Investigations
Allan B. Smythe
2009. ISBN: 978-1-60692-258-3

Mass Incarceration and Offender Reentry in the United States
Russell D. Javitze (Editor)
2009. ISBN: 978-1-60692-657-4

Batterer Intervention: Program Approaches and Criminal Justice Strategies
Kerry Healey, Christine Smith,and Chris O'Sullivan
2009. ISBN: 978-1-60692-934-6

Batterer Intervention: Program Approaches and Criminal Justice Strategies
Kerry Healey, Christine Smith and Chris O'Sullivan
2009. ISBN: 978-1-60876-537-9 (Online Book)

Digital Surveillance: Laws, Security and Related Issues
Joseph G. Massingale (Editor)
2009. ISBN: 978-1-60692-312-2

Incarceration and the Family: Issues, Effects and Approaches to Successful Reentry
U.S. Dept. of Health and Human Services
2009. ISBN: 978-1-60692-933-9

Policing the Police: Knowledge Management in Law Enforcement
Petter Gottschalk
2009. ISBN: 978-1-60741-765-1

Policing the Police: Knowledge Management in Law Enforcement
Petter Gottschalk
2009. ISBN: 978-1-60876-653-6 (Online Book)

Gun Ownership and the Second Amendment
Pjeter D. Baldrige
2009. ISBN: 978-1-60692-226-2

Homicide: Trends, Causes and Prevention
Randal B. Toliver and Ulrich R. Coyne (Editors)
2009. ISBN: 978-1-60741-625-8

Delinquency: Causes, Reduction and Prevention
Ozan Sahin and Joseph Maier (Editor)
2009. ISBN: 978-1-60741-558-9

Violent Crime and Prisons: Population, Health Conditions and Recidivism
Aidan Renshaw and Emelina Suárez (Editors)
2009. ISBN: 978-1-60741-668-5

Revisiting the Social Contract: Community Justice and Public Safety
Kathleen Auerhahn and Caitlin J. McGuire
2010. ISBN: 978-1-60876-446-4

CRIMINAL JUSTICE, LAW ENFORCEMENT AND CORRECTIONS SERIES

REVISITING THE SOCIAL CONTRACT: COMMUNITY JUSTICE AND PUBLIC SAFETY

KATHLEEN AUERHAHN
AND
CAITLIN J. MCGUIRE

Nova Science Publishers, Inc.
New York

For permission to use material from this book please contact us:
Telephone 631-231-7269; Fax 631-231-8175
Web Site: http://www.novapublishers.com

LIBRARY OF CONGRESS CATALOGING-IN-PUBLICATION DATA

Revisiting the social contract : community justice and public safety / editors, Kathleen Auerhahn, Caitlin J. McGuire.
p. cm.
Includes bibliographical references and index.
ISBN 978-1-60876-446-4 (pbk. : alk. paper)
1. Restorative justice. 2. Criminal justice, Administration of. 3. Social contract. 4. Public safety. I. Auerhahn, Kathleen, 1970- II. McGuire, Caitlin J.
HV8688.R498 2009
364.6'8--dc22

2009041954

Published by Nova Science Publishers, Inc. ✦ New York

CONTENTS

INTRODUCTION

In the criminal justice literature, "community justice" usually refers to a variety of alternative adjudicative strategies and practices. In this work, we suggest an additional conceptual formulation of community justice that emphasizes the role of the criminal justice system in providing *justice to communities*. Since the late twentieth century, the primary promise of the American criminal justice system has been to protect the public from dangerous offenders. This book evaluates contemporary incarceration policy and practice in the United States in light of that premise. The results indicate that criminal sentencing policy and practice have not succeeded in this aim; instead, a variety of evidence is presented that leads to the counterintuitive conclusion that rather than serving to reduce crime, mass incarceration is detrimental to public safety. This occurs as a result of both the failure of the criminal justice system to incapacitate the most dangerous offenders, and of the impacts on communities heavily impacted by incarceration policy. We conclude with a discussion of the meaning that these trends have for the concept of community justice, and suggestions for how consideration of the obligations of the social contract can and should improve outcomes in the criminal justice system and the communities affected by it.

Chapter 1

CRIMINAL JUSTICE AND THE SOCIAL CONTRACT

The problem is to find a form of association which will defend and protect with the whole common force the person and goods of each associate, and in which each, while uniting himself with all, may still obey himself alone, and remain as free as before.

Jean-Jacques Rousseau, 1762 [1968]

INTRODUCTION

Rousseau's classic depiction of the social contract recognized that individuals must sometimes surrender individual liberties in exchange for security provided by the government. In most modern democracies, individuals are willing to surrender liberties in exchange for the justice system's protection from crime. An implicit assumption of the social contract is that if an individual enters into such a contract with the justice system, he or she will be (at least to a reasonable extent) protected from criminal victimization.

Community justice models have powerfully altered this classic vision of the social contract. Instead of simply surrendering individual liberties in exchange for protection, community justice models require individuals to play a more direct role in the provision of their own safety. Community residents must express their priorities regarding protection and directly assist the justice system in creating safe communities by practicing informal social control. Under a community justice model, residents do not passively surrender individual liberties and automatically receive protection from victimization. Despite expectations for greater involvement from community residents, the community justice ideal still requires the formal criminal justice system to hold up their end of the bargain by delivering on residents' demands for public safety.

This book explores some of the ways in which the criminal justice system has failed to meet their obligations of the social contract. As one specific example, Californians have used referendum voting to express their desire to incapacitate the most dangerous criminal offenders. However, as the analyses in chapter 2 will demonstrate, the criminal justice system in California has not successfully carried out this mandate. In fact, these failed attempts at selective incapacitation have resulted in negative consequences both within the criminal justice system and within neighborhood social systems. At the state level, within the criminal justice system, the average level of dangerousness of individuals supervised in community settings has increased while the average dangerousness of the incarcerated population has declined. Additionally, we propose that the failures to meet the obligations of the social contract function at multiple levels of aggregation and perhaps even across levels. The failures of state-level sentencing policy and practice have had damaging effects at the neighborhood level. The extremely high rates of incarceration and reentry caused by state-level policies and practices have resulted in the disruption of neighborhood social networks, the inhibition of informal social control mechanisms, and a subsequent decline in collective efficacy in neighborhoods plagued by concentrated mass incarceration.

In this chapter, we will first review traditional conceptualizations of community justice and then argue for a reconceptualization of community justice that emphasizes the *obligations of the criminal justice system to communities.* In chapter 2, we examine some of the ways in which state-level policy and practice has not yielded the levels of public safety desired by community residents. The criminal justice system's failed efforts to incapacitate dangerous offenders have also translated into negative consequences for communities. In chapter 3, we will show that these failures have impacts on public safety at both the state level of the criminal justice system as well as at the neighborhood level. An understanding of these consequences will serve to supplement traditional models of community justice.

Traditional Conceptualizations of Community Justice

Although the interpretation of the community justice paradigm can be a source of disagreement among academics and practitioners, most community justice advocates agree that the term "community justice" can refer to a wide variety of ideals and practices (Clear 2007; Gilbert and Settles 2007; Clear and Karp 1998, 1999). Generally, community justice models emphasize the importance of making communities pleasant places to live, work and raise children (Clear 2007). The main focus of community justice programs is to enhance the quality of life for community residents (Clear and Karp 1999). It is important to point out that "quality of life" refers to a wide range of issues, including, but certainly not limited to, public safety (Smith 2001). Quality of life also includes how residents feel about their community and their willingness to contribute to community improvement endeavors.

Early conceptualizations by Clear and Karp (1999, 1998), pioneers of the community justice paradigm, emphasized four elements of community justice. First, Clear and Karp stressed the local nature of "community," maintaining that community justice functions at the neighborhood level. Local institutions and social relationships within a "place-based community" create the setting for community justice programs (Clear and Karp 1998: 14). Second, community justice embraces a problem-solving approach by relying on a proactive response to crime and social disorder in communities. As opposed to a "war on crime," crime is viewed as a societal problem that can be solved by tapping the resources of those directly affected by crime: offenders, victims, and community residents. By working together in a collaborative environment, strategies for preventing crime and social disorder can be developed. Third, community justice "decentralizes authority and accountability" (18). Clear and Karp provided the following examples of how community justice breaks down traditional hierarchies of power:

> new line authority in community policing often enables the cop on the beat to do much more than exercise enforcement powers. He or she is often able to organize community anticrime campaigns, mediate ongoing disputes, and coordinate the solution to problems by collaborating with workers from other agencies. Whether a social worker places an at-risk youth in a drug treatment program or a transportation planner alters traffic flow patterns through a highly visible drug market or "bazaar," the solution to any particular public safety problem will nearly always require inter-organizational integration (20).

Fourth, community justice models are characterized by the direct involvement of community residents. Citizen involvement is important not just for responding to crime, but also for building collective efficacy and reducing the potential for future crime. Strengthening collective efficacy will allow informal social controls in the community to "gradually share or even replace much of the formal justice apparatus" (Clear and Karp 1998: 15). Under community justice models, community residents must take responsibility for working collaboratively with law enforcement to address crime and social disorder problems.

Recently, researchers have attempted to more formally define community justice by identifying the key components of community justice initiatives. Most recently, Clear (2007) has highlighted three main characteristics of community justice. First, there must be an emphasis on *restoration*. Victims' property loss, sense of comfort and sense of control need to be restored through the community justice initiative. If offenders make amends for their offenses, their place (and status) in the community can also be reestablished. Additionally, it is important that a sense of "justice being done" exists in the community. Community members should feel like the harms caused by the crime have been sufficiently mended by any community justice process. Second, community justice models should emphasize the retention of offenders in the community as opposed to the removal of offenders through incarceration. Whenever possible, keeping offenders in the community will preserve existing social networks, which are of paramount importance to the development of collective efficacy, and the subsequent creation of conditions conducive to crime prevention. Third, sanctions which have an "ameliorative" or healing nature (such as community service, counseling sessions or substance abuse treatment) should be preferred over primarily punitive sanctions (such as incarceration).

Most importantly, in all conceptualizations of community justice, the relationship between community residents and the formal criminal justice system is key. Community justice requires a partnership between residents and justice system professionals. Particularly in neighborhoods with a history of distrust between residents and police, establishing such a partnership and maintaining the social contract has often proven quite difficult. Over a decade ago, Clear and Karp (1998) recognized that community involvement in the justice process and community cooperation with the formal justice system creates complex challenges for community justice. They noted that agencies are currently "experimenting" with different strategies to "formalize" the relationship between community members and the criminal justice system (19).

Clearly, distinctions between informal and formal social control are at the foundation of community justice conceptualizations. Informal social control occurs when an individual's behavior is regulated through interactions with family members, friends and local community members. Conversely, formal social control is characterized by behavior regulation from larger government bureaucracies, external to the individual such as law enforcement or the court system.

Considering the balance between informal and formal social control, it may be helpful to conceive of the relationship between community-based controls and the criminal justice system as a continuum, with total reliance on informal social control at one end, and complete reliance on the formal system of criminal sanctioning at the other. According to models of community justice which rely primarily on informal social control, community residents are primarily responsible for the prevention of and the response to crime and social disorder. At the opposite end of the continuum, there are community justice models which place greater reliance on the formal social control provided by the justice system.

Our conceptualization of community justice advocates community justice models that fall toward the middle of this conceptual continuum where both informal social control and formal social control play key roles in the prevention of and response to social disorder. Perhaps more importantly, we also recognize that few community justice models have sufficiently explored the *reciprocal* quality of the relationship between agents of informal social control and agents of formal social control. Particularly for community justice models that fall in the middle of the continuum and attempt to balance both informal social control from community members and formal social control from the justice system, it is crucial that both parties fulfill their required obligations. The following reconceptualization of the notion of community justice explores the ways in which the formal justice system fails to hold up their end of the bargain.

A Reconceptualization of Community Justice: The Breach of Contract

In this work, we argue for a reconceptualization and expansion of the notion of "community justice." While not disputing the importance of local communities in the production of justice and public safety, we argue that this cannot be separated from the context in which community justice processes operate -- i.e., the formal criminal justice system. It is neither possible nor desirable to "bracket" the existence of the criminal justice system from models of community justice. At the same time, it is not possible for the formal justice system to provide public safety without the cooperation of the local community. For this reason, we champion community justice models that occupy a middle ground on the conceptual continuum and seek to achieve the benefits that come from both informal and formal social control mechanisms.

While other conceptualizations of "community justice" have tended to focus on aspects of the criminal justice *process*, we present a formulation that emphasizes *outcomes* resulting from the operation of the criminal justice system, and the ways in which these relate to concerns of social justice. In the reconceptualization of community justice presented here, justice can be defined in terms of the criminal justice system operating in the manner in which community residents believe and wish it to – namely, by incapacitating dangerous offenders. This conception of "community justice" differs from more conventional uses of the term, which usually refer to alternatives to traditional criminal justice practice, particularly those that emphasize community residents' participation. These include community-based sanctions (such as intensive probation), community policing, citizens' watch groups, and sentencing circles (Clear and Karp 1999; Karp 1998). Although community justice models frequently advocate alternatives to incarceration and retaining offenders in community settings, few community justice supporters would dispute the fact that there are some extremely dangerous individuals who pose a significant threat to public safety if kept in the community.

In spirit, the notion of community justice we propose does not differ greatly from the ideas generally associated with it, at least in the sense that both arise out of frustration with the failures of the criminal justice system as it currently operates. This reconceptualization is not intended to replace or displace other usages, but rather to add another dimension to our understanding of the concept of community justice. Primarily, this reconceptualization is intended to draw greater attention to a crucial requirement of successful community justice programs: the need for the formal criminal justice system to fulfill its obligations to constituents, as required by the social contract. Indeed, Clear and Karp maintained that the justice system must be accountable to citizens, and the success of community justice endeavors can be evaluated in terms of citizens' satisfaction and perception that justice has been done (1998: 20-21).

In addition to emphasizing the formal justice system's breach of the social contract, our reconceptualization of community justice also advocates an expanded definition of "community." Existing definitions of community justice have tended to focus on the neighborhood level (Gilbert and Settles 2007, Clear 2007, Clear and Karp 1998). However, we propose that issues related to the partnership between the formal justice system and community residents should also be examined on a larger scale, such as the state level. There are a number of reasons that justify framing community justice within both the neighborhood level of aggregation and at higher levels of aggregation, such as counties, states, and even nations.

Community justice strategies have traditionally focused on neighborhoods because the types of crimes with which community justice has traditionally concerned itself (low-level social disorder problems such as prostitution, drug possession, public disorder, graffiti, and the like) register their impacts at the neighborhood level. Additionally, community justice strategies have been concerned with the neighborhood level because the social processes related to informal social control function at the neighborhood level. Social networks, an important precursor for the exhibition of informal social control, are fairly localized within communities. Traditional community justice conceptualizations, which heavily rely on informal social control, are focused on the neighborhood level because informal social control mechanisms are rooted in neighborhoods.

We assert that community justice principles can also be applied to the criminal justice response to larger criminal justice issues and serious crimes which are handled at the level of larger geographic units (i.e., counties, states, nations). The failure to incapacitate the most dangerous criminals who pose serious threats to public safety is an important problem that has implications for public safety at several levels of aggregation. Although it has effects on the neighborhood level, the formal criminal justice apparatus operates at the state level, not the neighborhood level. Because criminal justice policies are generally determined by state legislatures, the greatest amount of variation in criminal justice policy occurs between states, not within states. It is thus appropriate to consider larger geographical units as "communities" when considering the obligations of governments to provide safety and security in cooperation with the wishes of residents/constituents.

Although we conceptualize the possibility of community justice principles functioning at both the community level and the state level, it is also important to recognize that the balance between formal and informal social control likely varies depending on the level of aggregation. At the neighborhood level, where community justice typically addresses low-level social disorder problems, community residents play a *direct* role in crime prevention and responses to disorder. At the state level, in which there is greater concern for more serious offenses, residents play a more *indirect* role in crime prevention and responses to crime by communicating with formal agencies about their expectations for safety.

There is some support for our expanded conceptualization of "community" in the community justice literature, despite the traditional emphasis on the neighborhood level. For example, Bazemore (1998) recognized the flexibility of the term "community." He explained that

> [h]ow community is defined in justice decision making affects the nature and extent of citizen involvement and ownership... While each [type of community justice program] claims to increase the level of this involvement and ownership, practical agendas for doing so vary

> because conceptualizations of the 'community' differ... [T]he community and restorative justice movement has achieved little consensus on this issue. There is a tendency to talk about community in the macro or societal sense for some purposes, while defining community as those who 'show up' at a community sanctioning process for others (342).

Following Bazemore, Clear and Karp (1999: 40) noted that community can be conceptualized "without limiting it to geographic spaces." Rather, they argued that community should be thought of as an "entity" or a "quality of social existence: an indication of solidarity, shared practices and traditions, and emotional connectedness" (60).

In the case of California, discussed in the chapter that follows, it is appropriate to apply principles of community justice (mainly the importance of a partnership between the formal justice system and residents) to a state-level analysis because the social problem (incarcerating dangerous offenders) is one that is addressed at the state level, and, as will be shown, has consequences at the neighborhood level. The analyses presented in chapter 2 will demonstrate that the criminal justice system has not succeeded according to a community justice perspective because residents' demands for the provision of public safety through the workings of the apparatus of criminal punishment have not been met.

Although little empirical research is available on this point, our conceptualization of community justice also proposes the possibility of cross-level effects. State-level policies influence neighborhood-level incarceration rates. Neighborhood-level incarceration rates have effects on neighborhood-level social processes that relate to crime control. The analyses presented in chapter 2 empirically demonstrate the state-level effects of failed justice system efforts to protect communities. Chapter 3 explores the community-level effects of the justice system's failed efforts. Although we present these two aspects of the problem separately, we certainly encourage future research that can further assess the relationship between state-level policy, community-level social processes and public safety.

Chapter 2

THE SYSTEM'S FAILURE AT THE STATE LEVEL

CRIMINAL JUSTICE IN THE LATE MODERN ERA

In recent history, the enterprise of criminal justice has been defined by an emphasis on criminal *punishment.* The punishment of criminal offenders is generally justified with respect to four goals: retribution, deterrence, incapacitation, and rehabilitation (see Walker, 1991, for a more lengthy consideration of these purposes). While the sentencing of individual offenders may simultaneously serve several of these goals, it is possible to discern general *paradigms* of criminal sentencing associated with certain historical eras (Auerhahn 2003). The rehabilitative paradigm held sway from the time of the inception of the modern penitentiary in 1776 until the early 1970s. This was expressed across the nation in indeterminate sentencing policies which were designed to tailor treatment to individual offenders. Increasing rates of crime throughout the 1960s and 1970s, as well as a "radical loss of confidence in [American] political and social institutions" (Allen 1981:18) resulted in a reshaping of the discourse surrounding criminal punishment, particularly concerning the goals of incarceration. Evidence of this shift can be seen in the movement from indeterminate to determinate sentencing that took place throughout the United States in the 1970s (Auerhahn 2003: chapter 2; Hewitt and Clear 1983; Kadish 1978).

In the last three decades, sentencing policy reform in the United States has reflected an emphasis on the objective of *selective incapacitation* (Greenberg 1975; Greenwood with Abrahamse 1982; Zimring and Hawkins 1995). Reforms based on this idea promise to preserve public safety by incapacitating (via incarceration) particularly dangerous offenders for lengthy terms (see Auerhahn 1998 and 2003, chapter 4, for analysis and explanation of the operational problems with selective incapacitation). Nowhere is the prominence of the idea of the incapacitation of dangerous offenders through incarceration better exemplified than in California. In 1994, the state legislature signed into law the most inclusive and widely implemented Three-Strikes habitual-offender statute in the nation.[1]

Despite skepticism about the feasibility of selective incapacitation on the part of the criminal justice research community (Auerhahn 1998; von Hirsch and Gottfredson 1984; Blackmore and Welsh 1983; Cohen 1983), there is evidence that the emphasis on selective incapacitation is reflective of the wishes of the California electorate. While approximately half the U.S. states have some form of the ballot initiative process in place, no state's criminal justice system has been shaped more by ballot initiatives than California.[2] Since its introduction in 1911, the initiative process creates a direct connection between public opinion and criminal justice policy in the state. In the last three decades, a great deal of the state's criminal justice policy has been shaped by initiatives (see Figure 1). Between 1934 (the first time an initiative related to criminal justice appeared on the state ballot) and 1970, only three criminal justice-related initiatives appeared in state elections. Between 1970 and 2008, forty-one criminal justice initiatives – nearly all of which advocated harsher sentences and the building of more prisons – appeared on the California ballot.[3] The majority of these initiatives reflect an interest in the idea of selective incapacitation and a concern with public safety.

---

[1] California's "Three Strikes and You're Out" statute has a complicated legislative history. It was initially proposed to the state assembly by two democrats from Fresno, the home district of Mike Reynolds, father of infamous crime victim Kimber Reynolds, and was subsequently defeated in committee. The measure was later passed by the state legislature in March 1994. At the same time, a ballot initiative proposing a duplicate measure was already in the electoral process, and remained on the ballot for the November 1994 election, where it was overwhelmingly approved by the voters. The passage of the ballot initiative did not change the features of the law, but because it was now cemented by the ballot initiative, due to California legislative rules, either a two-thirds majority in the state legislature or another ballot initiative is required to alter or repeal the statute.

[2] Only a handful of states use ballot initiatives with some frequency. Interestingly, Western states are overrepresented in both groups – those with some form of ballot initiative as part of the governance process, and those that use it frequently.

[3] It should be noted that the majority of criminal justice-related ballot initiatives during the period of interest were initiated in the legislature, as opposed to grass-roots civic groups. However, popular support of these measures is evidenced by the voting majorities approving the various measures. Overall, approximately 80% of the criminal-justice related initiatives between 1980 and 2008 were voted into law.

Figure 1. Criminal Justice-Related Ballot Initiatives in California, 1934-2008.

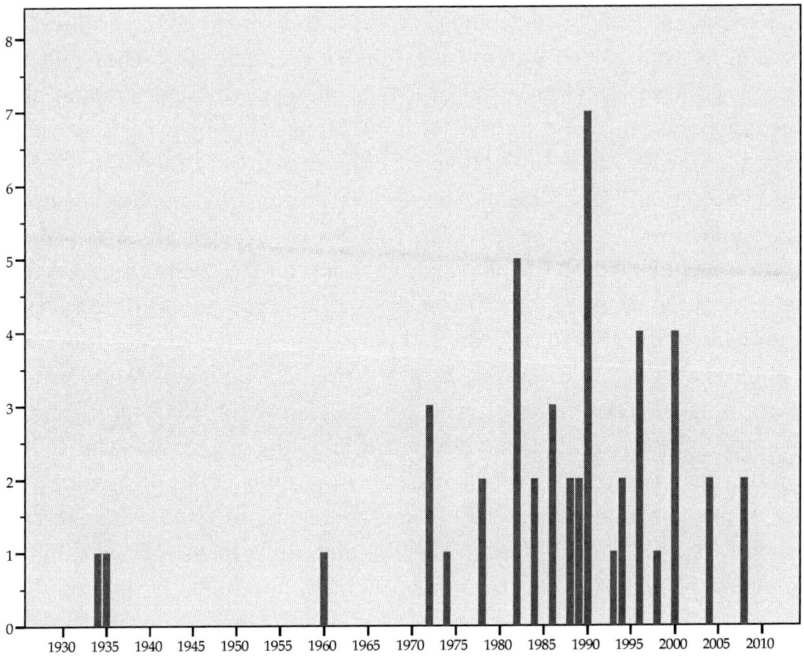

These include the 1982 "Victims' Rights Initiative," 1994's "Three Strikes and You're Out" law, and many – nearly one-third of the total number – were bond issues for prison and jail construction (see Jones 1998 and Auerhahn 2003, chapter 3 for a fuller discussion of the history of ballot initiatives in California's criminal justice system).

Between 1984 and 1996, twenty new prison facilities were built in California (California Department of Corrections and Rehabilitation 1995, 2000). This was made possible by the voters' approval of, on average, $500 million in general obligation bonds for new prison construction in each biennial election between 1982 and 1992. Interestingly, the political debate surrounding each of these ballot initiatives illustrated consensus regarding the value of incapacitation; conflict over the initiatives focused on differences of opinion about strategies for *financing* the construction of new prisons, rather than any question about the validity of the enterprise (Auerhahn 2003:52). Analysis of the ballot initiative process as a reflection of "community will" indicates that Californians wanted more prisons, and that they wanted them based on an expectation that building (and filling) more prisons would enhance public safety.

The purpose of the following section is to evaluate sentencing policy reform in California from the standpoint of selective incapacitation. This work differs from previous analyses of sentencing reform both in terms of the criteria used for evaluation, as well as the outlook that guides the analysis. The evaluation of sentencing policies based on a public safety or selective incapacitation objective has historically been made on the basis of crime-rate changes; however, given numerous criticisms and limitations of this work (see Auerhahn 1999 for a review), an approach grounded in the *selective success* of the policies is used here.

The notion of *selective success* represents a departure from the usual approach to the evaluation of sentencing policies and practices guided by the goal of the selective incapacitation of dangerous offenders. Focusing on changes in crime rates *assumes* that these policies operate as they are intended to – i.e., that the dangerous offenders ostensibly targeted by these policies are indeed selected and incapacitated, resulting in fewer crimes. However, there are a number of reasons to question this assumption, including the decreased sensitivity of a system that incarcerates an ever-increasing proportion of the population (Canela-Cacho, Blumstein and Cohen 1997), the problem of false-positive predictions (Auerhahn 1998, 2006; Monahan 1978), and the effects of substitution and criminal groups (Zimring and Hawkins 1995; Blumstein et al. 1978:65; Spelman 1994).

A criminal justice system functioning according to the principles of selective incapacitation should exhibit certain properties. If policies intending to achieve the selective incapacitation of dangerous offenders are successful, dangerousness should be maximized in incarcerated populations, and minimized in non-incarcerated populations. The empirical question this analysis seeks to answer, then, is this: has more than thirty years of sentencing reform intended to protect Californians – a great deal of which has been driven by the direct participation of California voters – been successful in this objective? Has the criminal justice system fulfilled its promises to the community?

Systems Analysis and Selective Incapacitation

Empirical research in criminology frequently tends to take the form of static or time-series analyses of single components of the system (e.g. jails, prisons, courts) rather than conceiving of the entire system *as a system* (important exceptions include Ohlin and Remington 1993; Blumstein and Larson 1969; Cassidy 1985; Cassidy et al. 1981; and Cassidy and Turner 1978) . However, legislative changes which are intended to influence one component of the system may result in unintended systemwide consequences. For example, the primary aim of California's 1994 Three Strikes law is the incarceration of "habitual offenders" for lengthy terms in prison. However, this law has had a dramatic impact on many other parts of the criminal justice system as well. The impact has also been seen in jails, where available space for sentenced offenders has been reduced due to an unprecedented increase in pretrial detention (Turner 1999). Trial volume has also increased, as defendants facing a second or third strike become increasingly unwilling or unable to plea bargain (LAO 1995, 2005; Zimring, Hawkins and Kamin 2001). Analyzing the impacts of legislative changes to sentencing structures from a systems perspective can provide important and useful insights into the unintended outcomes that result from these changes.

Systems analysis can be used to evaluate system performance in terms of its own explicit objectives – in this case, as defined by the citizens whom the system ostensibly serves. If the criminal justice system is operating according to principles of selective incapacitation, then custodial system populations such as prison and jail should exhibit a higher degree of dangerousness than non-custodial populations such as parole and probation.

Operationalizing Dangerousness

Dangerousness in criminal justice system populations is measured in this analysis by an additive index comprising multiple indicators of the correlates of what is universally considered dangerous criminal behavior (see Monahan 1981; Scott 1977; Chaiken and Chaiken 1982; Thornberry and Jacoby 1979; Steadman and Cocozza 1974). These include age, gender, length and nature of criminal history, and current offense (the coding scheme is given in Table 1). The measure is similar in structure to the Legal Dangerousness Scale used by Steadman and Cocozza (1974) in their study of the post-release outcomes of offenders designated as criminally insane. The measure consisted of information on juvenile criminal history, the number of prior incarcerations, presence or absence of violent convictions, and severity of the conviction offense (107). The researchers found that the combination of the offenders' age and his score on this simple four-item scale successfully distinguished between released patients who were rearrested and/or rehospitalized and those who were not (Steadman and Cocozza 1974:146-147).

Table 1. Coding Scheme for Dangerousness Measure.

Characteristic		Score
Age	18-24	4
	25-34	3
	35-44	2
	45-54	1
	55 and older	0
Gender	Male	1
	Female	0
Prior felony convictions	2	2
	1	1
	None	0
Prior violent convictions	1 or more	1
	None	0
Current conviction offense	Violent	3
	Property	2
	Drug	1

Minimum score: 1
(55 + year old woman, no priors, drug offense)
Maximum score: 11
(18-24 year old male, 2 or more priors, violent prior(s), violent offense)

This analysis differs from the work of Steadman and Cocozza in an important way, however, in that the assessment or prediction of dangerousness in individual offenders is *not* a goal of the research. The systems approach considers the relative dangerousness of criminal justice system populations in the aggregate as an indicator of the selective success of the criminal justice system. If sentencing policy reforms that aim to protect the public by incapacitating dangerous offenders have been successful, then the mean level of dangerousness should be highest – or at least show an increase over time – in the prison population. This relatively simple, unweighted measure is not intended to be to be the last word on the measurement of dangerousness in criminal justice system populations. It is intended to be used in a heuristic fashion to evaluate changes in the composition of criminal justice populations, both in terms of comparing different populations and in analyzing changes in a single population over time.

Figure 2. Structural Model of the California Criminal Justice System.

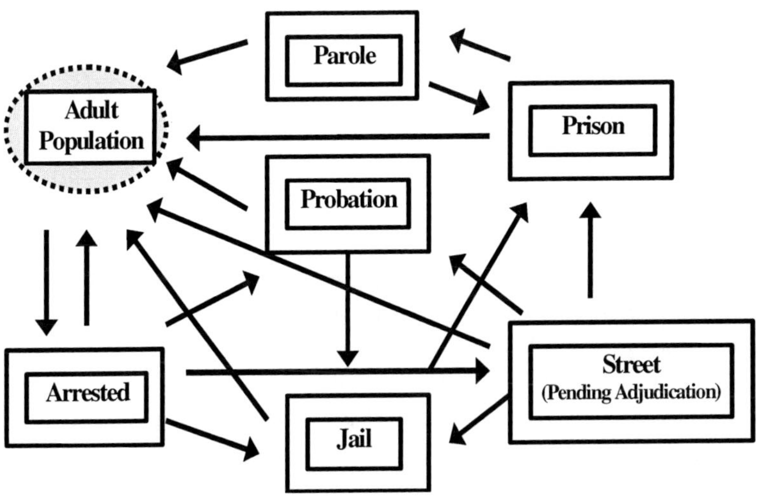

System Simulation

This analysis utilizes *data-validated dynamic systems simulation modeling* to evaluate the performance of California's criminal justice system with respect to the goal of selective incapacitation. This approach is based on the systems dynamics approach of Jay Forrester (1969) as explicated in Hanneman (1988). Berkeley Madonna software is used to codify the structural relationships among criminal justice populations (e.g. arrested, jail, prison, probation, parole). The model is initialized with values based on historical data, and then iterated over time to reproduce those data over the period 1980-1998.

The system is comprised of *states* and *rates*. The *states* are *population-states* occupied by individuals within the system. These include the arrested population, the jail population, and the prison population. Figure 2 is a simplified schematic of the systemic model. The complexity of the structural model places this analytic task beyond the capacity of statistical methods due to the problem of model identification.

The *rates* represent the probability of an offender moving from one state to another. The transition rates in the system are potentially dynamic, in that the simulation methodology allows for the modeling of the effects of feedback and informational processes on these rates at different points in time. The outcomes that result from the operation of the system, such as the size and composition of correctional populations, are the result of the movement of individuals through system states.

The system's structure is codified in the model as a series of differential and difference equations, which are initialized with values based on actual data and then iterated over time. The dynamic parameter values for each subgroup are finalized by altering parameter estimates and equations to fit the model output to the time-shapes of the historical data series for each system state over the time period that is the subject of the model.[4]

The system flows comprise the movement of individuals through the states of the criminal justice system. It is important to note that the models are not designed to describe the experiences of individual offenders, but rather to describe the compositional dynamics of system *populations*. The process of integrating system flows over time recognizes the fact that some of the elements of a criminal justice system population (e.g. prison) at year one are likely to be contained in that population at year two; therefore, the observations (prison, t1 and prison, t2) are *not* independent in the statistical sense. For this reason, the dynamic systems approach may be a more accurate way of modeling criminal justice system populations than are statistical approaches that assume the independence of observations.

---

[4] The simulation methodology can also be used to prospectively estimate the effects of continuing existing policy, or of policy changes, into the future. The plausibility of these projections is based on the accuracy of the data-validated stage of the modeling process, and the assumptions used to model policy changes. Interested readers are referred to Auerhahn (2002, 2003; 2004; 2008) for examples of prospective dynamic system simulation analyses.

The composition of a population state at time (t) is equal to the population at time (t-1), plus new arrivals, and minus exits. A single iteration of the model is conceived as a "time-step." The simulation modeling software does not itself specify the metric of the time-steps. For the models described here, the incremental unit of time is specified as one year. The analyst is free to define the unit of time (a week, a month, etc.) that best fits the specific problem of interest and the validation data available. System states are represented by differential equations, which take the general form of

STATE (T) = STATE (T-1) + (INFLOWS – OUTFLOWS) *DT

The composition of a population state at time (*t*) is equal to the population at time (*t-1*), plus new arrivals, and minus exits.[5] The inflows and outflows are described by rate equations, which represent the proportion of the "sending" state that moves into the "receiving" state at each time step. For example, the equation that models the prison population at time (*t*) takes the following form:

**PRISON (t) = PRISON (t-1) + ([(STREET (t) * prison commitment rate from STREET) + (JAIL (t) * prison commitment rate from jail) +
(PAROLE (t) * return rate)] - [(PRISON (t) * parole rate) + (PRISON(t) * unconditional release rate)]) *dt**

In this case, the inflows consist of new commitments to prison resulting from criminal convictions and recommitments resulting from parole violations. The outflows consist of parole releases and unconditional releases.

The rate equations are in turn modified by another quantity, which may accelerate or decelerate the rate over time. This elaborated form of the equation is

---

5 The model is structured such that the "arrested" population state clears on each iteration of the model. This means that 100% of the arrested population at t1 occupies a different state or leaves the model at t2. The general (non-criminal justice system involved) population is set up as a source/sink, as indicated here by the ellipse. In dynamic systems modeling, sources and sinks can be thought of as the boundaries of the model, in that they represent unlimited supplies of a particular input or resource (individuals who may become involved with the criminal justice system), and also serve as "absorbers" of resources as they exit the model (individuals leaving the criminal justice system by varied mechanisms such as charge dismissal, acquittal, or completion of probation or other sentences). Because of this, the equation generating the arrested system state takes a slightly different form than that of the other population states. A new arrested population is generated at each time-step by taking the initial value of the arrested population – in each of the 450 sub-models – and applying a multiplier to simulate growth or decline over time.

PRISON (t) = PRISON (t-1) + ([{(STREET (t) * prison commitment rate from STREET) * *street conviction rate modifier*} + {(JAIL (t) * prison commitment rate from jail) * *jail conviction rate modifier*} + {(PAROLE (t) * return rate) * *return rate modifier*}] - [{(PRISON (t) * parole rate) * *parole rate modifier*} + {(PRISON (t) * unconditional release rate) * *release rate modifier*}]) *dt

Each transition parameter is regulated over time by an informational quantity or multiplier. If a particular transition probability remains constant over time, the value of this multiplier is set to equal one. In the case of declining rates over time, multipliers have values lower than one. This technique is truly dynamic, in that the simulation methodology allows for the specification of nonmonotonic functions, whereby rates may change over time – using delay functions, "shocks," or decay processes. The most common specification used in the current analysis is a delay function characterized by a rate of increase at time (t) through (t+X), and a greater rate of increase for the time period after (t+X).[6]

Offenders move from one criminal justice system state to another at different rates. A number of factors that influence transition probabilities within the system are legally relevant, such as prior criminal record or type of conviction offense. Other factors that influence transition probabilities include gender, age, and race (Irwin 1985; Gorton and Boies 1999; Crawford, Chiricos and Kleck 1998; Tonry 1995; Bridges and Crutchfield 1988). In order to accurately reproduce system dynamics, the simulation modeling process must take into account variables that are known to influence transition probabilities. This necessitates the construction of a number of structurally equivalent models for individuals with similar groupings of attributes. The attributes accounted for in the models are: age (in groups 18-24, 25-34, 35-44, 45-54, and 55 and older), race/ethnicity (White, Black, Hispanic), gender, number of prior felony convictions (0, 1, 2 or more), the presence or absence of a violent felony conviction, and current conviction offense (drug, property, violent). The matrix representing every possible combination of these six attributes results in 450 population subgroups (e.g. 18-24 year old White male; one prior, violent prior, drug offense), for which the structural model depicted in Figure 2 must be separately (but simultaneously) estimated. For ease

6 In modeling the system, a remarkable amount of consistency was observed in the timing of these changes. The "switching point" for many of the rate modifiers – at all levels of the system, from arrest through incarceration – lay in the time period between 1985 and 1987. This should not come as a terrific surprise to anyone with even a cursory understanding of the history of American criminal justice policy reform as relates to sentencing.

of visualization and analysis, these 450 sub-models are then compiled to represent the system as a whole.

The transition probabilities represent the proportion of the "sending" population that exits that state at each iteration of the model. Generally, the transition parameters for each population subgroup are not known. In most cases, a baseline (average) transition probability can be obtained simply by dividing the size of the sending population by the size of the receiving population. In the absence of any theoretical justification to do otherwise, start values for transition probabilities for each of the 450 groups were assigned at this baseline, and altered in the course of model specification to reproduce system dynamics as represented by the validation data. For certain transition pathways, the receiving state has more than one contributing state. In the case of the transition rates that give rise to jail populations, the base rates are calculated by taking into account the relative proportions of sentenced and pretrial offenders in the population and pro-rating the relevant transition pathways to reflect these proportions.

Unique transition probabilities for different subgroups may be estimated in certain cases. When unique probabilities can be reasonably estimated from detailed validation data using the division method, these are applied for the relevant population subgroups. The data on prison and parole populations are the most complete with respect to model attributes, so the parameters for transition between these two states, and those for prison release rates were initialized uniquely for each population subgroup.

Different transition probabilities are also specified when theoretical justification exists for doing so. For example, with respect to the initial values of the transition probabilities for pretrial release and pretrial detention, it is well-established that nonwhite, male, younger, and violent offenders are more likely to be detained prior to adjudication than are white, female, older, and nonviolent offenders (Bridges and Crutchfield 1988; Crawford et al. 1998; Gorton and Boies 1999; Irwin 1985; Petee 1993; Steury and Frank 1990).[7] The initial transition probabilities are set for each population subgroup in a way that reflects the patterns demonstrated in the research literature. The dynamic parameter values for each subgroup were finalized by visually fitting the model output to the time-shapes of the actual data for each sub-model, as well as for the compiled series.

---

[7] Explaining these differences, while a worthwhile endeavor, is beyond the scope of this analysis. Many researchers do attempt to explain them (e.g. Bridges and Steen, 1998; Irwin, 1985; Meyers, 1987; Swigert and Farrell, 1976; Farrell and Holmes, 1991), and the reader interested in the reasons such differences exist is referred to these authors. For our purposes, these differences are merely noted as "social facts" and incorporated into the modeling strategy in an effort to reproduce system dynamics as accurately as possible.

VALIDATION DATA

Yearly data on adult felony arrests for the period 1979-1998 were provided by the California Department of Justice, Criminal Justice Statistics Center. Detailed data on jail and probation populations were somewhat more difficult to obtain. Limited data on these populations are available from the California Department of Justice (1980-1997), and more specific values for each of the 450 relevant subgroups were estimated, based on the patterns of representation in the arrest data. Data on prison and parole entrances, exits, and daily population over the period 1979-1998 were provided by the Research Bureau of the California Department of Corrections (CDC).

Results[8]

The fulfillment of the community justice ideal as it is here conceived would require that the criminal sanctioning system in California operate according to the principles of selective success – i.e., the maximization of dangerousness in custodial criminal justice populations relative to non-custodial populations. It is apparent that this did not take place in California between 1980 and 1998. As Figure 3 indicates, while the prison population was nearly the most dangerous of the criminal justice system populations in 1980 (the probation population had a dangerousness value that was minutely larger than that of the prison population). After 1980, this was no longer the case. The probation population was the most dangerous criminal justice system population over the entire period. Indeed, after 1980, the probation population was, on average, 32% *more* dangerous than the prison population, and 35% more dangerous than the jail population.

The arrested population was less dangerous throughout the series than all other criminal justice system populations, except parole. This is as it should be, as the process of arrest would seem to exhibit the least selectivity. Arrest casts the widest net; the system should subsequently filter and select more serious offenders for sanctions. However, comparing the dangerousness levels in the arrested population and the jail population indicates that the jail population was, on average, only marginally more dangerous than the arrested population. In

8 Widely accepted goodness-of-fit measures for simulation models are lacking. In the present analysis, a target of no more than 10% deviation of all simulated series from the validation data was established; the simulation results for all system states met this standard. Space limitations

1980 the jail population was actually 4% *less* dangerous than the arrested population, and thereafter exhibited a dangerousness level approximately 2% greater than that of the arrested population.

Figure 3. Relative Dangerousness of Criminal Justice Populations, 1980-1998.

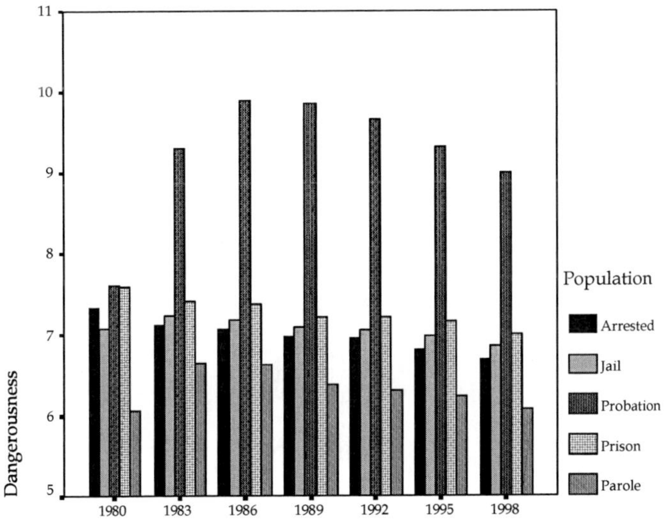

Even more striking, the prison population was also only marginally more dangerous than the arrested population during this period. Overall, the prison population was only 4% more dangerous than the arrested population during the twenty-year period analyzed, indicating a lack of selective success.

The prison population was at all points more dangerous than the parole population. This is consistent with the successful implementation of selective incapacitation policies, but the difference in dangerousness between the two system populations over the time period analyzed is not large. While the prison population was 25% more dangerous than the parole population in 1980, the gap between the two narrowed thereafter, with the dangerousness of the prison population averaging only 13% more than that of the parole population.

The finding that *probation* was the most dangerous system population is clearly at odds with the notion of community justice put forth in this work. The push to "get tough" in California has resulted in an expansion of the penal system

prevent us from reproducing those results here. The interested reader is referred to Auerhahn (2003; chapter 7) for detailed results of the entire simulated system.

the likes of which is unprecedented anywhere in the world. Between 1984 and 1996, the state of California built (and filled) twenty new prison facilities (California Department of Corrections, 1995, 2000); it has been estimated that the bond initiatives approved by the voters to fund this spree will ultimately cost Californians over $5.2 billion (Davis 1995). The state's nonpartisan Legislative Analyst's Office (LAO) estimated in 1997 that the state would need to construct fourteen new prisons just to relieve existing overcrowding (LAO 1997). The new Kern Valley State Prison was opened in 2005. In addition, since 2006 the California Department of Corrections and Rehabilitation (CDCR; the word "rehabilitation" was added to the agency's title in 2005) has housed inmates out of state "for the purpose of temporarily alleviating overcrowding within existing institutions" (CDCR 2008). The agency currently contracts with the Corrections Corporation of America to operate six facilities in four states (CDCR 2008).[9] What all this prison construction has ostensibly "bought" is safer streets – yet the most dangerous offenders are on the street rather than in prisons. To further examine these issues, we turn to a detailed comparison of the prison and probation populations.

PRISON

Over the period of study, the average dangerousness of the prison population declined 8%, from a high of 7.58 in 1980 to a low of 7.01 in 1998 (Figure 4). This decrease can be explained primarily by the aging of the prison population over this period, and by the increase in drug offenders relative to other offenders. While the youngest offenders (those aged 18-24) comprised 31% of the prison population in 1980, only 22% of the prison population was under 25 in 1998. Similarly, while less than 25% of the prison population was 35 or older in 1980, more than 40% of prisoners were older than 35 in 1998.

Even more remarkable are the changes in the distribution of conviction offenses in the prison population during this period. In other criminal justice system populations during this period we observe a pattern of change that appears to be a trading-off between drug and property offenses, with the proportion of violent offenses remaining relatively constant. However, the change in the

[9] In February 2009, a three-judge panel of federal judges ordered the state to reduce the prison population by 55,000 inmates in order to meet constitutional standards for the provision of health care services. At the time of this writing, state officials plan to appeal the decision to the United States Supreme Court.

distribution of offenses in the prison population between 1980 and 1998 follows rather a different pattern. The proportion of *property* offenses remained relatively constant over this time period – around 25% of the prison population – but the proportion of violent offenders declined sharply. Violent offenders comprised nearly two-thirds of prisoners in 1980, but by 1998 less than half of the prison population were offenders serving a sentence for a violent conviction offense. In 1980, barely 10% of California prisoners were incarcerated on a drug offense; by 1998, this figure was over 30%.

Figure 4. Dangerousness of Prison Population, 1980-1998.

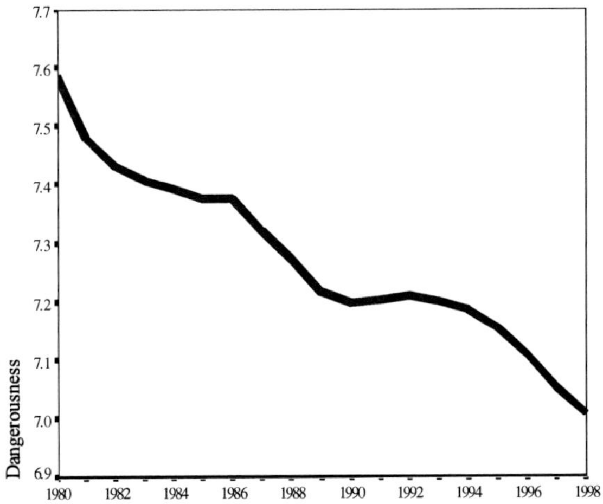

Table 2. Offense Composition of California Prison Population, 1980-1998.

Year	Prison Population	Drug	Property	Violent
1980	20,248	.10	.26	.64
1985	52,849	.21	.29	.49
1990	94,184	.28	.26	.45
1995	136,216	.31	.25	.45
1998	155,937	.32	.24	.44

Table 3. Age Composition of California Prison Population, 1980-1998.

Year	18-24	25-34	35-44	45-54	55 and older
1980	.31	.47	.16	.05	.02
1985	.33	.40	.16	.07	.04
1990	.27	.44	.19	.06	.04
1995	.23	.41	.25	.08	.03
1998	.21	.37	.28	.10	.03

Table 4. Racial/Ethnic and Gender Composition of California Prison Population, 1980-1998.

Year	White	Hispanic	Black	Male	Female
1980	.42	.24	.35	.95	.05
1985	.41	.23	.36	.94	.06
1990	.37	.26	.37	.93	.07
1995	.37	.31	.32	.93	.07
1998	.37	.32	.31	.92	.08

Table 5. Criminal History Composition of California Prison Population, 1980-1998.

Year	Violent	Non-Violent	No priors	1 prior	2 or more priors
1980	.35	.65	.40	.50	.11
1985	.42	.58	.36	.44	.20
1990	.38	.62	.37	.41	.22
1995	.39	.61	.33	.41	.26
1998	.38	.62	.34	.39	.27

The proportion of prisoners with lengthy criminal histories (two or more prior convictions) sharply increased, to more than double 1980 levels in 1998; this increase in more-dangerous offenders mitigates the impact of the demographic changes on the declining dangerousness of the prison population. This increase is clearly *not* attributable to the 1994 Three Strikes law, as the trend in the series predates the law's passage. While the relative proportion of violent and nonviolent offenders in the prison population has demonstrated some minor fluctuation over time, the distribution of offenders by violence history remained essentially unchanged over the period.

Figure 5. Dangerousness of Probation Population, 1980-1998.

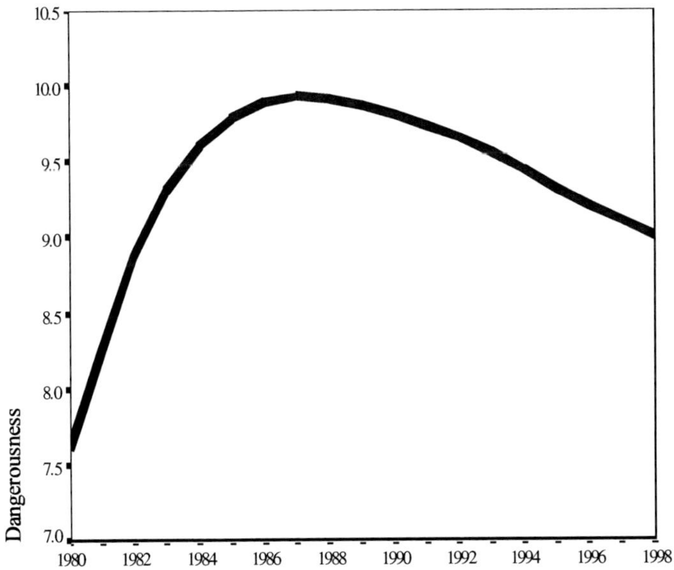

Probation

Figure 5 indicates that the probation population has become increasingly dangerous over time. The dangerousness level of the probation population peaked in the latter half of the 1980s and declined thereafter, but remained at a higher level than that of the early part of the 1980s. In quantitative terms, the dangerousness of the probation population increased 31% between 1980 and 1987, and declined 9% between 1987 and 1998. The net change in the dangerousness of the probation population from a value of 7.6 in 1980 to a value of 9.01 in 1998 is an increase of 19%. Possible explanations for this increase in the dangerousness of the probation population may lie in the changes in sentencing policy combined with capacity limitations in jails that occurred throughout the 1980s. As penalties for drug offenses became increasingly harsh, a trade-off relationship may have developed whereby less dangerous drug offenders occupied available jail space (either as pretrial detainees, due to the perception of flight risk, or as sentenced offenders), resulting in more dangerous offenders who might have otherwise received a jail sentence being placed on probation.

Table 6. Offense Composition of California Probation Population, 1980-1998.

	Violent	Property	Drug
1980	.25	.36	.39
1985	.29	.30	.41
1990	.29	.25	.46
1995	.33	.22	.45
1998	.34	.21	.45

Table 7. Age Composition of California Probation Population, 1980-2000.

	18-24	25-34	35-44	45-54	55+
1980	.53	.30	.10	.04	.03
1985	.50	.34	.09	.03	.03
1990	.47	.37	.11	.03	.03
1995	.42	.37	.14	.03	.03
1998	.38	.37	.17	.04	.04

Table 8. Racial/Ethnic and Gender Composition of California Felony Probation Population, 1980-1998.

	White	Black	Hispanic	Male	Female
1980	.50	.21	.29	.75	.25
1985	.50	.28	.22	.83	.17
1990	.48	.28	.24	.83	.17
1995	.48	.25	.27	.82	.18
1998	.50	.22	.28	.79	.21

Table 9. Criminal History Composition of California Felony Probation Population, 1980-1998.

	Prior Convictions			Prior Violent Convictions	
	None	1	2 or more	None	1 or more
1980	.90	.10	.00	.98	.02
1985	.56	.20	.23	.82	.18
1990	.52	.22	.27	.79	.21
1995	.51	.20	.29	.78	.22
1998	.50	.20	.30	.78	.22

Examination of the components of the dangerousness construct seems to support this interpretation. The distribution of conviction offenses in the probation population changed dramatically over the two decades analyzed. While drug offenders comprised the greatest fraction of the probation population over the entire period, the relative positions of property and violent offenders flipped. Since 1980, the proportion of violent offenders in the probation population increased 36%, while the proportion of drug offenders increased only 15%, and property offenders as a share of the probation population declined 38%. Changes in the age distribution of the probation population have been minimal, and are not in a direction that would contribute significantly to the increased dangerousness of the probation population.

The proportion of probationers with histories of violence increased 20% from 1980 to 1998; this is consistent with the increase in probationers with violent conviction offenses. Another disturbing finding is an increase in the proportion of probationers with multiple priors, which is also consistent with the displacement scenario outlined above.

Systems Analysis and Community Justice

From the standpoint of selective incapacitation, the results of the retrospective evaluation of the selective success of the California criminal justice system are uniformly disappointing. The dangerousness of incarcerated populations has decreased rather than increased in the last two decades, while the dangerousness of non-custodial populations has either remained relatively constant, as in the case of parole, or increased dramatically, as in the case of probation.

It is apparent that the system as a whole is not effectively keeping pace with the massive influx of drug offenders that began in the mid-1980s. Most disturbing is the pattern of change in the distribution of conviction offenses in the prison population. While in other criminal justice system populations there appears to be a process of substitution of drug offenders for property offenders, in the prison population, the proportional representation of property offenders has remained relatively constant over the period 1980-1998. What has instead happened in the prison population is the displacement of violent offenders by drug offenders. These displaced violent offenders increasingly appear in non-custodial criminal justice system populations, notably probation.

This analysis highlights the importance of analyzing criminal justice reforms from a systemic perspective. The increased dangerousness of non-custodial populations, combined with the decreased dangerousness of custodial populations is an extremely important finding, in light of considerations of community justice. When considering the explicit aims of the system – the selective incapacitation of dangerous offenders – it is clear that the policy changes implemented during the 1970s, 1980s and 1990s were unsuccessful. Considering the actions of the criminal justice system as a response to the wishes of the community is also indicative of failure. The citizens of California have authorized the expenditure of a great deal of money to support and grow a criminal justice system that has extended certain promises – namely, the provision of safety. While the decrease in dangerousness of the prison population is not large, it assumes a greater significance in light of the two decades of sentencing policy reform primarily directed at increasing the public safety through the incapacitation of dangerous offenders, and the more than four-fold expansion of the prison population that took place during this period. While the vast majority of criminal justice reform in the past two decades has been directed at altering the composition of the prison population via the selective incapacitation of dangerous offenders, the analyses reported here demonstrate that these reforms have far-reaching effects on other areas of the criminal justice system, such as the jail and probation systems, often in ways that are inconsistent with the provision of justice to communities.

Chapter 3

THE SYSTEM'S FAILURE AT THE NEIGHBORHOOD LEVEL

UNINTENDED CONSEQUENCES AT THE NEIGHBORHOOD LEVEL: COERCIVE MOBILITY THEORY

In addition to the failure of the criminal justice system to incapacitate the most dangerous threats to communities, the damage to community social networks that results from these failed efforts represents an additional example of how the justice system has failed to uphold the social contract with its citizens. The previous chapter demonstrated the ways in which California residents have voiced their desire to be protected from the most dangerous criminals. The analyses in chapter 2 demonstrated that the formal justice system has failed to incapacitate the most dangerous criminals and has thus not provided the desired levels of protection from crime. This chapter will explain how the state level failures have not only represented failures in *formal* social control, but also have had detrimental effects on *informal* social control at the community level. State-level efforts to incarcerate the most dangerous criminals have translated into astronomically high rates of incarceration in disadvantaged communities. In these neighborhoods, where residents are attempting to use informal social control to address crime and disorder problems, the removal of community residents through incarceration damages local social networks. Without strong social networks, the ability of communities to exert informal social control is rather limited.

The theory of "coercive mobility," first articulated in 1998 by Dina R. Rose and Todd R. Clear, offered a new perspective on the relationship between formal criminal justice system interventions and crime control at the community level.

The conventional view of this relationship is that the removal of offenders from communities through incarceration will result in lower rates of crime (whether through the mechanism of deterrence, incapacitation, or rehabilitation). However, Rose and Clear proposed that "state social controls... have important secondary effects on family and neighborhood structures" (1998: 441). These effects, they argued, may have the counterintuitive result of *increasing*, rather than decreasing crime in communities heavily impacted by incarceration. Removing offenders from communities through incarceration may actually increase community crime rates.

A thorough understanding of the social processes theorized by coercive mobility requires an understanding of the social ecological research in which coercive mobility theory is rooted. Drawing upon a large volume of theoretical and empirical work in the ecological tradition, Rose and Clear noted that much is known about the relationships between community ecological characteristics and processes and the spatialized incidence of crime. Social disorganization theorists have observed that crime is more likely in communities that have weak or absent informal controls – in essence, crime is encouraged in communities that lack the capacity to effectively regulate the behavior of residents (Shaw and McKay 1942; Sampson 1987; Sampson and Groves 1989; Wilson 1987; Bursik 1988; Bursik and Grasmick 1993). Sampson, Raudenbush and Earls (1997) coined the term *collective efficacy* to refer to the capacity of neighborhoods to monitor and regulate undesirable behaviors; in this sense, collective efficacy can be thought of as the opposite of social disorganization.

Coercive mobility theory is essentially an expansion of collective efficacy theory that takes into account the effects of mass incarceration and high rates of re-entering prisoners on communities. Sampson, Raudenbush and Earls claimed that collective efficacy "depends on mutual trust and solidarity among neighbors" and refers to the "willingness of local residents to intervene for the common good" (1997: 919). Taylor (2001) enumerated the following features of neighborhoods characterized by high levels of social disorganization (or low levels of collective efficacy): residents do not get along with one another, residents do not belong to community organizations so they cannot work together to solve common problems, residents do not agree on what is acceptable behavior, and residents are unwilling to intervene if they witness someone misbehaving. Clearly, the social processes associated with collective efficacy are heavily dependent on relationships between community residents and the resulting social networks (Gibson, Zhao, Lovrich and Gaffney 2002; Morenoff, Sampson and Raudenbush 2001; Veysey and Messner 1999; Bellair 1997).

It is important to point out that collective efficacy has been measured or defined in a variety of ways. Some of the most common variables used as indicators of collective efficacy include informal social control, willingness to intervene, social cohesion and trust (Sampson et al. 1997). Notably, many of these concepts overlap with one another and measure similar social processes within neighborhoods, but the importance of conceptual distinctions certainly requires further investigation (Taylor 2002). Despite the issues with respect to discriminant validity (see Taylor 2002), a good deal of solid research has confirmed that neighborhoods with higher levels of collective efficacy experience lower rates of crime (Sampson, Raudenbush and Earls 1997; Sampson and Groves 1989; Taylor 2001; Bellair 1997).

Coercive mobility theory suggests that the potential for residents to exert informal social control or develop collective efficacy can be disrupted by high rates of incarceration and reentry. Rose and Clear proposed that "offenders have complex relationships" within their communities (1998: 442). Offenders may play both positive and negative roles in various community contexts. In addition to their criminal activities, individuals may also be active fathers, sons, workers, members of church congregations, and the like. By removing these offenders from their communities through incarceration, social networks – a critical component in the development of crime-reducing community processes, such as collective efficacy – are damaged.

Just as importantly, offenders acquire a variety of disadvantages while incarcerated, including the experience of a prison culture rooted in aggression, emotional distance and violence. Formerly incarcerated individuals eventually return to their communities with these disadvantages and then struggle to play a positive role in social networks, and subsequently the development of collective efficacy. Ex-offenders who return to communities often "cycle" back and forth between the community and prison. These "quasi-permanent prisoners" are not likely to stay in neighborhoods long enough to build and maintain the stable social networks that are required for effective informal social control (Clear 2007: 59). The theory of coercive mobility questions the effects that excessive use of formal social control (incarceration) can have on the potential for informal social control and subsequently on neighborhood crime rates.

It is important to note that the theory of coercive mobility does not predict a single, invariant relationship between incarceration/reentry rates and community crime rates. Rather, the theory proposes that this relationship depends on a number of conditions. Communities characterized by already high levels of collective efficacy are more likely to experience a net benefit as a result of the removal of predatory criminals; in areas with strong social networks and effective community controls, the removal of members – even if they are contributing in both positive and negative ways to the community – is less likely to cause severe disruption. In such communities, social networks can maintain social control despite the removal of some individuals. However, in neighborhoods characterized by high levels of social disorganization, and by definition, low levels of collective efficacy, informal social controls and networks are likely to be more tenuous, and therefore more easily damaged by the disruption resulting from community members' removal. Put another way, Rose and Clear suggest that "in disorganized areas with low levels of control partly due to weak [network] ties, the contribution of offenders may not be that much less than their nonoffending neighbors" (1998: 453). In such neighborhoods, the removal of offenders can have a very unsettling effect on social networks and a negative effect on the subsequent ability of community residents to exert informal social control.

Another important consideration for the relationship between incarceration and neighborhood crime rates is the level of incarceration to which a community is subject. It is well known that some communities are more heavily impacted by formal social controls than others. A number of studies have confirmed the concentration of high incarceration rates in certain communities. A landmark study on the neighborhood effects of incarceration and reentry conducted by Gottfredson and Taylor (1988) found that out of a total of sixty-six Baltimore neighborhoods, two of these neighborhoods contained over one-tenth of all men released from state correctional facilities. Using an alternative methodological strategy, Lynch and Sabol (2004a) found that in some Baltimore neighborhoods, nearly one-fifth of the male residents are absent as a result of incarceration. Similarly, in many sections of Brooklyn, New York, Clear and Cadora (2001) discovered that one out of every seven males between the ages of twenty and forty-five are incarcerated. Furthermore, Clear and Cole (1997) report that, over 90% of prisoners are released back to their communities, on average, within two years of admission. Such high rates of incarceration (and subsequent reentry) are certainly not characteristic of all neighborhoods, but rather, are concentrated in certain neighborhoods. The theory of coercive mobility proposes that incarceration will have the intended negative effect on crime only until incarceration rates reach a certain "tipping point" (Clear 2007: 164). Once incarceration rates rise to such a high level that social networks are severely disrupted by the removal of community members, the direction of this relationship will reverse and increasing incarceration rates will actually increase crime rates.

In many disadvantaged inner-city communities, high rates of incarceration and reentry negatively affect the local economy, disturb family life and, most importantly, disrupt social networks, all of which diminish the ability of residents to exert effective social control. Informal social control mechanisms are believed by many scholars to be much more important in maintaining order in a community than are the actions of the formal criminal justice system (Hunter 1985; Clear 2007; Sampson, Raudenbush and Earls 1997). Therefore, increasing incarceration rates in already disadvantaged neighborhoods may increase crime rates in these neighborhoods by reducing the capacity for neighborhoods to regulate themselves. The following analysis will summarize evidence of the ways in which the formal criminal justice system has failed to help communities exert informal social control.

Empirical Tests of Coercive Mobility Theory: The Relationship between Incarceration and Crime

In attempting to test the model of coercive mobility, researchers have frequently tested two sets of relationships separately: (1) the relationship between incarceration rates and crime rates and also (2) the relationship between incarceration rates, neighborhood-level social processes associated with collective efficacy, and crime rates. Unfortunately, little research has successfully attempted the ambitious task of testing the full coercive mobility model. Nonetheless, a review of the research on these separate relationships can provide partial support for coercive mobility theory and will certainly demonstrate the negative consequences of mass incarceration in certain communities.

The strongest tests of coercive mobility theory recognize the temporal dimension of the theory; that is, as incarceration and reentry rates rise *over time*, the effect of incarceration on crime rates will change. Much of the work that has used a longitudinal design has only tested the relationship between official incarceration rates and crime rates, while neglecting the intervening effects of neighborhood social processes, such as collective efficacy. This limitation is primarily a practical one. It is much easier to obtain official data on incarceration and crime rates over an extended period of time than it is to include data on social processes over time, which often require detailed surveys or interviews with neighborhood residents. Nonetheless, an examination of the research on the longitudinal relationship between incarceration and crime rates can provide partial support for the coercive mobility model. If there is no evidence that rising incarceration rates are associated with declining crime rates, such a null finding may be due to the damage caused to social networks by mass incarceration. If it were found that incarceration rates are associated with a decline in crime rates only until incarceration rates reach a certain level, this would provide further support for coercive mobility theory's concept of the "tipping point."

Some of the early research on the relationship between incarceration and crime reduction found that increasing incarceration rates had the intended negative effect on crime rates. Marvell and Moody (1994) reported that each additional individual imprisoned eliminates approximately seventeen index offenses.[1] Conversely, and in at least partial support of coercive mobility theory, more recent research has found that there is no clear relationship between rising incarceration and declining crime. Using data from fifty-eight Florida counties between 1980 and 2000, Kovandzic and Vieratis (2006) failed to identify a statistically significant relationship between prison population growth and crime rates over time. Although the direction of the coefficients indicated that a rising prison population may be related to declining crime rates, none of these relationships were statistically significant over time. The researchers proposed that perhaps there may have been initial deterrent or incapacitation effects (as evidenced by lower crime rates), but that these effects did not covary with prison populations. In other words, any deterrent or incapacitation effects on county crime rates did not depend on the size of the county prison population.

Research on the relationship between incarceration and crime rates has been characterized by many methodological disputes about the appropriate modeling of this relationship. The "endogeneity problem" characterized some of the earliest concerns among researchers and was successfully addressed in Levitt's (1996) work. Research on the relationship between crime and incarceration rates must determine the effects of incarceration on crime *independent* of the effects of crime on incarceration. If crime rates increase, it is logical that incarceration rates will also increase. This area of research is really interested in the subsequent effects that incarceration rates have on crime rates over time. Levitt overcame the endogeneity problem by including an *instrument* in his analyses; an instrumental variable is related to the independent variable (incarceration rates), but unrelated to the dependent variable (crime rates). The instrument employed by Levitt was court-ordered reductions in prison populations due to overcrowding. Levitt's state-level analyses between 1971 and 1993 showed that states that were not required to shorten sentences to comply with court-ordered prison population reductions had lower crime rates than states that were forced to shorten sentences. According to Levitt, these findings provide evidence that incarceration is

[1] Estimates of individual offending frequencies exhibit a great deal of variability, with reported values ranging from 2 to 187 offenses per year (see Spelman 1994:71-80, and Auerhahn 2003:60-71, for a comprehensive review).

associated with reduced crime rates, even after accounting for the endogeneity problem.

Although Kovandzic and Vieratis (2006), Levitt (1996) and Marvell and Moody (1994) accounted for the temporal aspect of coercive mobility theory, these studies still failed to appropriately model the nature of the relationship between incarceration and crime rates. Clear (2007) and Rose and Clear's (1998) coercive mobility theory suggested that previous studies testing a *linear* relationship between incarceration rates and crime rates are incorrect. According to coercive mobility theory, this relationship is *curvilinear*; that is, incarceration rates will be associated with decreased crime rates until a "tipping point" at which additional increases in the incarceration rate will no longer decrease crime rates.

Spelman (2000) agreed with Rose and Clear that the relationship between incarceration and crime is likely not linear. Using data from previous studies, his analysis revealed the possibility that the effect of incarceration on crime may vary depending on the scale of incarceration. In other words, the elasticity – the percentage change in the crime rate that is caused by a one percent increase in the incarceration rate – may not be the same for all incarceration rates. However, Spelman's regression analyses did not support Rose and Clear's expectations. As the prison population increased, the positive effect on crime also increased. Rising incarceration rates continued to reduce crime rates even as the prison population increased.[2]

Since the suggestion by Rose and Clear (1998) of a potential curvilinear relationship between incarceration and community crime rates, other studies have refuted Spelman's findings. Liedka, Piehl and Useem (2006) argued that Spelman's model was methodologically flawed, due to the inclusion of only a single quadratic function of the imprisonment variable. In so doing, the only possible outcomes that could be found were that incarceration rates either increase or decrease crime rates at a decreasing rate. Liedka et al. argued that a properly estimated model would include both a linear term and a quadratic term in order to explore a wider range of potential relationships between the incarceration rate and the crime rate. Significant findings with a linear term would indicate that there is a one-directional relationship between incarceration and crime rates (i.e., incarceration either causes an increase or decrease in crime). Significant findings with a quadratic term could denote a curvilinear relationship between

[2] However, it is important to point out that Spelman also concluded that the crime rate would have declined in the 1990s regardless of the increase in the prison population. He attributes this to the changing age structure of the population (fewer individuals in the most crime-prone years) and improved policing strategies.

incarceration and crime rates (i.e., low levels of incarceration may decrease crime, but high levels of incarceration may increase crime). However, if *both* linear and quadratic terms were found to be significant, this could indicate a relationship between the two characterized by a threshold effect such as that predicted by Rose and Clear, whereby incarceration decreases crime up to a certain level, but after a certain "tipping point," the direction of the relationship reverses.

Liedka et al. (2006) first specified what they labeled the "less-less hypothesis," which can be thought of as a relationship of diminishing returns (248). The *less-less* relationship occurs when rising incarceration rates begin to have a weaker effect on crime as the incarceration rates grow. In other words, the percentage reduction in crime rates caused by incarceration rates is less when incarceration rates are already high. On the other hand, the *crime-augmentation hypothesis* predicts that additional increases in incarceration will actually have a positive effect on crime rates. As incarceration rates increase, crime rates will also increase because the "social damage of high rates of imprisonment outweighs the crime reduction effects" (249).

Employing models including both linear and quadratic terms, Liedka et al. used state prison population data and Uniform Crime Report data from 1972-2000 to examine the relationship between incarceration levels and crime rates for all fifty states and the District of Columbia. When attempting to predict crime rates using state prison populations, both their linear and quadratic models provided evidence for the *less-less hypothesis.* When incarceration levels were low, increasing incarceration rates were associated with decreasing crime rates over time. However, in states with already high rates of incarceration, further increases in incarceration rates were associated with *increased* crime over time. More specifically, in the quadratic lag models, at the median value of the state prison population, a ten percent increase in the prison population yielded lower crime rates by approximately one percent. At the twenty-fifth percentile of the prison population, a ten percent increase in imprisonment rates reduced crime by 1.25%. However, at the seventy-fifth percentile of the prison population, a ten percent increase in imprisonment reduced crime by only .36%. Clearly, the scale of imprisonment does "matter" (245).

Also seeking to improve on methodological limitations of previous work, Renauer, Cunningham, Feyerherm, O'Connor and Bellatty (2006) responded to Rose and Clear's (1998) test of the curvilinear relationship between incarceration rates and crime. To test this relationship, Rose and Clear used negative binomial regression, which applies a log transformation to the dependent variable. However, as Renauer et al. recognized, log transforming a dependent variable when an expected relationship is curvilinear can result in an improperly specified model (see Hannon and Knapp 2003). To address this potential misspecification, Renauer and colleagues used three different estimation techniques to test the relationship between incarceration and crime rates in ninety-five Portland neighborhoods. Although Renauer et al. expected the heteroskedasticity consistent covariance (HC3) model to be the most accurate, the results were quite similar for the HC3 model, the model using traditional ordinary least squares regression and the negative binomial regression model also used by Rose and Clear. All three models showed support for a curvilinear relationship between incarceration rates and *violent* crime rates, but all three failed to find any significant relationship between incarceration rates and *property* crime rates.

Although research on the relationship between incarceration and crime has been subjected to numerous methodological disputes, such research has provided some support for the notion that high rates of incarceration (and, by implication, reentry) can have the counterintuitive result of increasing crime in communities heavily affected by mass incarceration. This next section will examine research that attempts to test a more complete model of coercive mobility theory by taking into account neighborhood social processes affected by the removal of community residents, (and by their reintroduction through reentry) that influence community crime rates.

Empirical Tests of Coercive Mobility Theory: The Relationships between Incarceration / Reentry Rates, Neighborhood-Level Social Processes and Crime Rates

Rose and Clear (1998) were among the first to suggest that *formal* social control could play a role in the production (or hindrance) of collective efficacy. Rose and Clear emphasized that the prior assumptions of social disorganization theory indicated that: (1) high levels of social disorganization (or low collective efficacy or low private controls) predicted increased crime and (2) high levels of formal, public control (such as incarceration) predicted decreased crime. Rose and Clear theorized that increased public control may inhibit private controls, resulting in increased crime.

Gottfredson and Taylor (1988) were the first to test the effects of reentry rates on neighborhood social processes, including processes associated with collective efficacy. This study relied on both official data for crime rates and release rates as well as survey and interview data for information on neighborhood-level processes. Examining Baltimore neighborhoods to which men were returned from state institutions between 1978 and 1982, they found that residents in neighborhoods with high concentrations of released offenders were more likely to report high levels of anomie, incivilities and crime. While prior research had found that neighborhood socio-economic status, stability, ethnicity and age predicted community level outcomes, Gottfredson and Taylor's study confirmed that neighborhood concentrations of released offenders added explanatory power to models predicting community-level outcomes. More specifically, the rate of released offenders accounted for an additional fifteen percent of the variance explained in predicting residents' perceptions of crime as a neighborhood problem, thirteen percent of variance explained when predicting residents' reports of restricted activity and an impressive twenty percent of the variance explained when predicting actual neighborhood crime rates.

Gottfredson and Taylor's work certainly established the existence of relationships among high rates of returning offenders, social processes associated with high levels of social disorganization (or low levels of collective efficacy) and high crime rates. Despite the methodological strengths of their work, this study cannot be considered a complete test of coercive mobility theory. The primary weakness of this study in relation to coercive mobility theory is that it cannot demonstrate causality or track trends over time. For coercive mobility theory to be validated, a study would need to demonstrate the following causal model: high rates of released individuals caused negative neighborhood processes (anomie, incivility, poor perceptions of the neighborhood) and that incarceration/reentry rates and these negative neighborhood processes both caused crime rates to rise over time.

In an effort to qualitatively explore the effects of high incarceration rates on community social processes, Clear, Rose and Ryder (2001) conducted in-depth interviews and focus groups with thirty-nine residents (including a small number of ex-offenders) in areas heavily impacted by incarceration in Tallahassee, Florida. Notably, these authors reported that "in the focus groups and individual interviews, respondents devoted more time to describing the negative effect of incarceration than the positive, and their passions seemed to be more readily engaged by these issues than the traditional matters of public safety" (340). Their findings substantiated and illuminated those of Gottfredson and Taylor regarding the impact of reentry on social and community processes. Their investigation revealed that interpersonal networks are severely damaged by high rates of incarceration and reentry. Respondents reported that relationships with neighbors are disrupted because neighbors become fearful of families who have an incarcerated family member. Relationships within families are also disrupted, often due to the significant economic loss caused by removing the income contribution of the incarcerated individual, as well as the economic burden resulting from supporting the incarcerated family member following release. Additionally, when ex-offenders return to communities, "neighbors are welcoming but cautious, suspicious and frequently fearful" (342). In sum, Clear et al. (2001) found that relationships between neighborhood residents and within families are damaged by both the removal (incarceration) and return (reentry) of individuals.

Clear, Rose, Waring and Scully (2003) later confirmed the qualitative findings in Tallahassee with official data on crime rates, department of corrections admissions and releases, and U.S. Census data on race, residential mobility, and socio-economic status. Although their study was not able to investigate changes over time, the Clear et al. (2003) study did confirm that incarceration and release rates impacted crime rates in the manner hypothesized by coercive mobility theory. While controlling for variables related to collective efficacy, their results indicated a curvilinear relationship between incarceration and crime rates.

It should also be recognized that Clear et al. (2003) attempted to use socially meaningful neighborhood boundaries. Local neighborhood associations were asked to describe the boundaries of their association and these descriptions were paired with police-reporting areas. Although some boundary descriptions fell outside of the Tallahassee study area and the research team was forced to drop these areas from the analysis, the remaining neighborhoods at least represented geographic units that were likely to be more meaningful to community residents than census tracts or block groups.

The delineation of neighborhood boundaries is a reoccurring and certainly very important issue in multilevel research on neighborhoods. Social ecology researchers have wondered whether different strategies for defining neighborhood boundaries can have misleading influences on a particular outcome (see Wooldredge 2002). One perspective maintains that neighborhood social processes occur within socially meaningful units. That is, residents are aware of neighborhood boundaries because social processes vary significantly between these neighborhoods. If the goal is to create neighborhood boundaries that represent consequential between-group differences, then neighborhoods should be defined by residents themselves. On the other hand, some neighborhood-level research is less concerned with whether or not there is any social meaning behind how geographic areas are defined. For these researchers, the variation between areas is acceptably significant even when using neighborhood boundaries that are not determined by organic social processes, such as census tracts or counties.

In partial support of both of these perspectives, a good deal of research has found that different characteristics of social ecology and different social processes may function at different levels of aggregation. Studies exploring potential aggregation bias have found that some neighborhood variables influence an outcome at one level of aggregation and other neighborhood variables influence the same outcome at a different level of aggregation. For example, Rountree and Land's (1996) study found that levels of social integration predicted residents' perceptions of crime risk at the street block level and that income levels predicted risk perceptions at the census tract level. Although disputes over aggregation bias will surely continue, the main lesson of multilevel neighborhood research should be that the choice of geographic units should be based on theoretically meaningful considerations. As Wooldredge (2002:685) speculates about Rountree and Land's findings, perhaps street blocks are the best level of aggregation for variables related to neighborhood identification (such as social integration) while "indicators of ecological dynamics under systemic models may operate at broader (parochial) levels." In reference to Clear et al.'s (2003) study, the decision to use neighborhood boundaries that are meaningful to neighborhood residents makes sense in light of their theoretical expectations for how social processes function within communities.

Although they did not thoroughly consider the possibility of aggregation bias, Lynch and Sabol (2004b) have conducted one of the most complete tests of the relationship between incarceration rates, neighborhood social processes and crime rates. Using Taylor's (2001) survey data on individuals in thirty Baltimore neighborhoods, Lynch and Sabol made an important methodological contribution to the literature by using three different types of models: single-equation ordinary least squares (OLS) modeling, structural equation modeling (SEM), and hierarchical linear modeling (HLM) to investigate the relationship between informal social control and incarceration rates.

According to the OLS results, there were only two variables that had significant (and positive) effects on residents' willingness to engage in informal social control (an important aspect of collective efficacy): residents' feelings of community solidarity and the degree to which residents were "neighborly". Contrary to what would be expected by coercive mobility theory, changes in incarceration rates over time did *not* influence residents' willingness to engage in informal social control.

The use of SEM represented a methodological improvement over the OLS models because they were able to parse out indirect effects. The SEM results were consistent with the OLS findings in failing to find a direct relationship between incarceration rates and informal social control. However, in support of coercive mobility theory, increases in incarceration negatively impacted social processes that are related to informal social control, such as community solidarity.

odels showed that increases on community solidarity. effects on informal social p between incarceration rates rcive mobility theory.

lyses were also used in order to Considering the nature of the data ded a more accurate model of outcomes to separate individual-level effects and to these models, changes in prison admission with community solidarity. Most important in heory, there was a direct and positive effect of cial control. Rising crime rates were also associated nity solidarity. Such findings are particularly interesting "support the common belief that incarceration promotes ation through crime reduction," but rather that "increasing obilize communities" (Lynch and Sabol 2004b: 158).

rk by Mears, Wang, Hay and Bales (2008) has also contributed an piece to the literature on the relationship between incarceration rates, hood processes and crime rates. Coercive mobility theory proposes that gative effects of high incarceration rates are a result of *both* the removal and ntry of community members. Clear (2007) asserted that returning ex-offenders to communities with all of the economic and social deficits associated with being an ex-offender is simply "piling on the collateral consequences" (58). In light of the importance of reentry in coercive mobility theory, Mears and colleagues have pointed out that there has been a lot of research on how social ecology affects crime, but little research on how social ecology affects reentry success. In other words, perhaps reentry is relevant to community crime rates because neighborhood social processes may predict whether returning individuals reoffend.

Studying nearly 50,000 men returning from prison to sixty-seven Florida counties, Mears and colleagues found that released prisoners who return to resource-deprived areas are significantly more likely to be reconvicted of a violent crime. They also confirmed their hypothesis that the effect of resource deprivation on likelihood of recidivism would be greater for young, non-white males compared to other age and racial groups. Such findings on the role of resource deprivation at the community level is applicable to the current examination of collective efficacy because socio-economic status has repeatedly been identified as an indicator of social disorganization, which can be thought of

as the opposite of collective efficacy (Sampson and Gro
Messner 1999; Sampson, Raudenbush and Earls 1997; Shaw

Mears and colleagues' study only examines the likelihoo
based on an *indicator* of collective efficacy (resource deprivat
study is certainly a step in the right direction because of the
reentry rates, future research should attempt to parse out the like
success based on actual neighborhood social processes that charac
efficacy. For example, a study could investigate how the likelih
success varied based on the degree to which neighborhood residen
(and able) to participate in informal social control. Such a study ma
demonstrate *why* a high rate of returning ex-offenders has negative co
for communities' crime levels and whether a community's level of
efficacy can *mediate* the negative effect of reentry on community crime.

Empirical tests of the idea that high rates of incarceration and reentry
social networks and the ability of residents to develop collective efficacy
yielded mixed results. Generally, research conducted by Rose, Clear
colleagues has found support for coercive mobility theory. However, o
research has found that high rates of incarceration are not necessarily associa
with damaged social networks, collective efficacy, or higher crime rates under a
circumstances (Lynch and Sabol 2004a; Lynch, Sabol, Planty and Shelly 2002).

Prison Places: The Interaction of Race/Ethnicity and Community in Coercive Mobility

Considering the mixed results in studies of coercive mobility theory, some researchers have proposed that perhaps another variable – race and ethnicity – may account for some of these mixed findings. The effects of mass incarceration and high rates of reentry are more pronounced in some neighborhoods than others. Using the term "prison places" to describe impoverished, inner city, predominantly minority neighborhoods with a disproportionate rate of entries to and exits from prison, Clear (2007: 67) emphasized that incarceration rates vary by geographic location, residents' race/ethnicity and residents' socio-economic status.

Race/ethnicity and place also appear to be closely related when identifying "prison places" with particularly high rates of incarceration and reentry. Comparisons of White and Black neighborhoods in Brooklyn have demonstrated how race/ethnicity and place interact when examining mass incarceration. Clear and Rose's (2003) analysis of Brooklyn neighborhoods estimated that in predominantly Black communities, the incarceration rate is approximately twelve per one thousand residents. Conversely, in neighborhoods with predominately White residents, the estimated incarceration rate is less than three per one thousand residents.

Evidence of high rates of incarceration concentrated in certain neighborhoods indicates that informal social control will be particularly difficult to exert in these neighborhoods. The following section will detail how constant disruption to social networks caused by the repeated removal and return of ex-offenders in neighborhoods of mass incarceration can actually increase crime rates in these neighborhoods.

Piquero, West, Fagan and Holland (2006) were the first to test for racial/ethnic variation in the relationship between incarceration and neighborhood-level factors related to the creation of safe communities. Hypothesizing that the "community consequences of incarceration are racialized," Piquero et al. tested the nature of the relationship between incarceration rates in New York City census tracts and two neighborhood-level variables: median income and human capital (257).

It is important to understand how these two variables relate to coercive mobility theory. Median income was likely chosen as a proxy for socio-economic status, which has traditionally been used as an *indicator* of social disorganization and collective efficacy (Shaw and McKay, 1942; Sampson and Groves, 1989; Veysey and Messner, 1999; Lowenkamp, Cullen and Pratt, 2003). Piquero et al. measured human capital as a scale including educational attainment, labor force participation, and job skills. According to Clear (2007: 76), human capital refers to the "personal resources an individual brings to the social and economic marketplace." Human capital, in turn, is necessary for the development of social capital. Much like collective efficacy, social capital represents the ability of residents to "call upon personal ties (usually within social networks) in order to advance some personal interest," including controlling dangerous criminal behaviors in their community (Clear 2007: 80).

Conducting separate regression models for Blacks, Hispanics, and Whites and other races combined, Piquero and colleagues were first able to confirm Clear's (2007) depictions of "prison places" by finding that Blacks and Hispanics had higher rates of both prison and jail admissions than Whites/Others during the period of study, between 1985 and 1996. In the predictive analyses for Blacks, neighborhoods with higher prison admissions of Blacks were associated with lower median incomes and lower levels of human capital. Contrary to expectations, higher drug arrest rates were associated with higher median incomes. However, as predicted by coercive mobility theory, higher drug arrest rates and homicide victimization rates were both associated with lower levels of human capital. And partially consistent with coercive mobility theory, higher levels of informal social control or supervision were associated with higher human capital, but lower median incomes.[3]

For the Hispanic analyses, neither jail or prison admissions was associated with Hispanics' median income. However, higher jail admissions were related to lower human capital. As predicted, higher drug arrest and homicide victimization rates predicted lower median incomes and human capital. Also as predicted, greater social control or supervision was associated with greater median income and human capital.

It is important to note that in the research conducted by Piquero and colleagues, an individual who was *not* Black or Hispanic (classified in the research as White/Other) was admitted to a jail in only 7.2% of all census tracts examined. The corresponding figure for prison admissions was 8.2%. For Whites/Others, jail admissions predicted lower median incomes, but not lower human capital. Prison admissions failed to significantly predict either median income or human capital for Whites/Others. Higher homicide victimization and drug arrest rates were associated with lower median income and human capital. And similar to Blacks, more social control or supervision was related to greater human capital, but lower median income.

Piquero and colleagues thus confirmed their hypothesis that the effects of incarceration on neighborhood characteristics do vary by race/ethnicity. They concluded that, "incarceration, then, does not appear to exert deleterious consequences among Whites/Others, at least with regard to the two measures of neighborhood well-being assessed herein" (268). Such findings provide support for Clear's (2007) and Clear and Rose's (1998) assertions that the negative effects of incarceration on social networks are most severely experienced in already disadvantaged minority neighborhoods.

[3] Such a finding may be caused by the fact that human capital is a better proxy for the actual processes related to collective efficacy than median income. While median income is only an *indicator* of collective efficacy, human capital is closer to representing the actual social processes of collective efficacy.

COERCIVE MOBILITY, COMMUNITY JUSTICE AND PUBLIC SAFETY

Clearly, in many disadvantaged communities, the formal criminal justice system has failed to meet their obligations under the social contract. While the research results reported here are somewhat mixed, there is an accumulating body of evidence that concentrated, mass incarceration has caused serious problems for many communities. Instead of making communities safer, mass incarceration has, in some communities, disrupted social networks and inhibited the ability of residents to exert informal social control – resulting in communities that are *less* safe as the result of the actions of the criminal justice system.

Within the framework of coercive mobility theory, first articulated by Rose and Clear (1998) and subsequently expanded and refined in Clear (2007; with Rose and Ryder, 2001; with Rose, 2003; with Rose, Waring and Scully, 2003), the negative effects of mass incarceration are understandable. In communities most damaged by these "side effects" of formal criminal justice system intervention, the influence of coercive mobility of community residents on local-level social processes is complex: "not only do disorganized communities have more networks disrupted through incarceration, the impact may be stronger in these neighborhoods because they have a lower threshold due to depleted supplies of social capital" (Rose and Clear, 1998: 457).

Although residents have sought to create safe communities through the use of informal social control, such efforts have been negated by the excessive use of formal social control. By repeatedly removing and returning individuals from their communities, the formal criminal justice system has severely disrupted the social networks that are required for communities to effectively control behavior in their neighborhoods.

Chapter 4

RECONCEPTUALIZING COMMUNITY JUSTICE

> *A promise underlies public policy: if the actions we recommend are undertaken, good (intended) consequences rather than bad (unintended) ones will actually come about.*
>
> Aaron Wildavsky, 1979

The concept of community justice is an important one for contemporary criminal justice. Although traditional conceptualizations of community justice have focused on neighborhood-level initiatives and processes, in this work, we have demonstrated that the notion of community justice can and should be expanded to encompass the ideas of the social contract and the obligations that the formal criminal justice system has to provide or foster public safety in communities.

This reconceptualization is in no way at odds with traditional conceptualizations of community justice that focus on alternatives to the formal criminal justice system. It remains a fact that even if such alternatives proliferate and augment the activities of state-level sanctioning systems, the sanctioning of offenders will continue to be a necessary component of governments' responsibility to protect citizens from serious criminal victimization. That being said, the wider community – that which exists both within and beyond the neighborhood level – can and should participate in the process of the provision of public safety at all levels of the sanctioning system, holding governments accountable for their successes or failures in this objective. This reconceptualization is intended to draw greater attention to a crucial requirement of successful community justice programs: the need of the formal criminal justice system to fulfill its obligations to constituents, as required by the social contract.

The most prominent promise made by the criminal justice system is the provision of safety. In recent decades, this has been focused, operationally, on the use of incarceration to remove dangerous individuals from communities. The analyses of the California criminal justice system reported in chapter 2 indicate that the system has faltered miserably on this promise. Despite an emphasis in sentencing policy on the incarceration of dangerous offenders, what has in fact happened in California is a redistribution of offenders such that the most dangerous offenders are now to be found in community correctional settings, while the average dangerousness of the prison population has declined.

With more than 2.3 million adults incarcerated in state prisons, federal prisons, and jails, the United States leads the world in both the number of prisoners and the percentage of population incarcerated. This comes at an enormous price, both in terms of the financial cost of incarceration, as well as the opportunity costs of this social policy choice. The Pew Center on the States (2008) reported that the cost of incarcerating offenders in state prisons in 2007 exceeded $44 billion, representing a 315% increase over prison spending in 1987. The authors of the report noted that "[a]djusted to 2007 dollars, the increase was 127 percent. Over the same period, adjusted spending on higher education rose just 21 percent" (Pew Center on the States 2008:3). Only five U.S. states spend as much on higher education as they do on corrections (Pew Center on the States 2008: 16).

The combination of overreliance on incarceration and the abandonment of post-release supervision and support has also had the effects of degrading community-level processes related to informal social control that are central to the creation and maintenance of safe communities. Approximately 95% of prisoners are eventually released; nationwide, over 600,000 offenders re-enter communities each year. Recent trends in get-tough crime policy, such as the abolishment of parole, result in many of these offenders being released with no supervision and little to nothing in the way of support services. In light of these trends, it is unsurprising that rearrest rates for offenders within three years of release increased between 1983 and 1994 (Hughes and Wilson 2009).

As we have shown through our examination of the evidence supporting the theory of coercive mobility in chapter 3, the removal and re-introduction of these offenders has detrimental effects on community crime rates. The potentially negative effects of high incarceration and reentry rates for communities is largely rooted in social ecological theory, namely social disorganization and collective efficacy theories. These theories propose that community crime rates are highest in neighborhoods with low levels of collective efficacy. In neighborhoods with low levels of collective efficacy, residents do not get along with one another, they do not belong to community organizations so they cannot work together to solve common problems, they do not agree on what is acceptable behavior and they are unwilling to intervene if they witness someone misbehaving (Taylor 2001).

Clear and Rose were the first to suggest that high rates of incarceration and reentry at the neighborhood level might negatively influence the social processes related to collective efficacy. Although traditional viewpoints on the relationship between incarceration and crime assume that increasing incarceration rates will decrease crime rates, coercive mobility theory proposes that this relationship is not invariant. Social networks play an important role in whether or not a community can build and maintain the capacity to control behaviors within the community. The repeated removal and return of offenders to certain communities over time can have detrimental effects on social networks and, subsequently, increase community crime rates.

The negative effects of formal social control on informal social control function through both the mechanisms of removing community residents (through incarceration) and the reintroduction of ex-offenders (reentry). Although a particular community resident may participate in criminal activities, it is also likely that the individual participates in positive activities within the community, such as being a father, employee, or religious leader. By removing this individual from the community, the positive social networks in which this individual is involved may be disrupted. In turn, the damaged social network may struggle to exert informal social control within the community. Additionally, when individuals return to their community, they bring with them the many disadvantages of being an ex-offender, including the stigmatizing "convict" label and the internalization of a prison culture. Such conditions pose challenges for building the social networks that are required for informal social control.

Importantly, coercive mobility theory is proposed to apply only in particular situations: when neighborhood crime rates reach a particular "tipping point" and in neighborhoods with already low levels of collective efficacy. In neighborhoods where incarceration and reentry rates are not very high and where community residents already have fairly stable social networks, the removal and return of individuals is less damaging to communities. However, in neighborhoods that are already plagued by mass incarceration, high reentry rates and already have low levels of collective efficacy, the removal and return of additional individuals can have harmful effects on community-level processes that serve to reduce crime.

The potentially negative effects of formal social control have important implications for our reconceptualization of community justice that emphasizes the responsibility of the formal criminal justice system to hold up its end of the social contract. If community residents are attempting to work together to keep crime rates low through the exertion of informal social control, the formal criminal justice system should not interfere with these efforts through the mechanisms of mass incarceration and subsequent reentry. For this reason, it is essential that the concept of community justice be expanded to take into account the will of community members (however defined) in setting policy and practice in the criminal justice system.

In addition to minimizing the formal justice system's over-reliance on mass incarceration, we would like to propose several additional strategies for improving informal social control in communities. Despite the detrimental effects on processes of informal social control caused by the over-reaching of the formal justice system, some efforts can still be undertaken to advance informal social control.

First, mechanisms within communities that can facilitate the development of informal social control must be enhanced. Opportunities for residents to join local neighborhood improvement associations and participate in community service projects need to be expanded. Unfortunately, these endeavors are frequently limited by the lack of financial support for these associations and projects. Although government funding for these kinds of social programs is always limited, we have demonstrated in this work that an astronomical amount of money is going to waste on both new prison construction and the maintenance of mass incarceration. The reallocation of a mere fraction of the corrections budget to support neighborhood associations could likely reduce crime in neighborhoods by encouraging – instead of inhibiting – the development of informal social control mechanisms and processes.

Second, ex-offenders must play a direct role in informal social control within communities. The LIFERS (Long Incarcerated Fraternity Engaging Release Studies) organization at Graterford State Correctional Institution in Pennsylvania has offered a powerful explanation of how transformed ex-offenders can play a prominent role in neighborhood crime reduction (2004). LIFERS is a nonprofit corporate organization comprised of men serving life terms at the Pennsylvania State Correctional Institution at Graterford, located approximately thirty miles to the north and west of Philadelphia. In existence since 1980, the initial purpose of the organization was to pursue legislative reform regarding Pennsylvania's policy of no parole for life-sentenced prisoners. However, in the early 1990s, the LIFERS expanded their mission to include "a stronger emphasis on civic and personal responsibility, and crime prevention" (2004: 52s).

One of a number of anti-crime initiatives undertaken by the organization, the LIFERS Public Safety Initiative "was launched as a movement designed to help the public recognize the culture of crime and engage citizens to work toward eliminating it" (LIFERS Public Safety Steering Committee 2004: 49s). The Public Safety Initiative proceeds from the understanding that

> As a tradition, crime-fighting efforts have been, and remain, unidirectional, that is, proceeding from local, state, or federal law enforcement agencies who assume the responsibilities for solving crimes and creating laws and policies designed to safeguard average citizens. Oftentimes, communities in which most crimes occur are only nominally incorporated in crime-fighting efforts, and government agencies assume the bulk of these responsibilities in the name of the public. (49s).

In addition to pointing out the lack of general community involvement, the LIFERS Public Safety Initiative Steering Committee further stresses the insufficient involvement of ex-offenders in community crime control. Specifically, they propose that when formerly incarcerated individuals return to their communities, they should devote themselves to ending what they have labeled the "culture of street crime." According to the members of the Steering Committee of the Public Safety Initiative (2004), individuals who engage in criminal behaviors value a particular set of principles, norms and behaviors. The following statement explains their theory of the culture of street crime as a primary cause of criminality:

> Notwithstanding racism and economic factors, it can be reasonably argued that a high rate of crime in wealthy industrialized nations is symptomatic of a society suffering from moral malnutrition. Criminals on every level of society become addicted to the psychological sweets derived from engaging in antisocial behavior. Much of the crime and violence in society can be directly linked to the inculcation of sociopsychological behavioral responses to feelings of anger, fear, shame, deprivation, entitlement, and greed. The practice of selective morality through a process of circumstantial rationalization has become commonplace, among criminals and those working to decrease or control crime levels. Habitual criminals become desensitized to the adverse effects their actions have on the

> lives of their victims and society, not to mention their own families and loved ones (56s).

The involvement of ex-offenders in ending this culture of street crime is essential, in the view of the members of LIFERS because they have "the experience, knowledge, insight, and expertise" to help draw young people from the criminal lifestyle (65s).

Ex-offenders become equipped to help others escape the culture of street crime not through externally-imposed rehabilitation while incarcerated, but rather through an internal process of *transformation* that powerfully alters how ex-offenders view the world and their role in it. Although transformation essentially comes from within, "the process that begins with the self ends with the transformation of others" (64s). Upon return to the community, transformed ex-offenders can play a role in crime prevention by working with at-risk youth and confronting those engaged in the culture of street crime.

The LIFERS recognize that the implementation of their plan will require not only ex-offenders, but also the cooperation of "academics, penologists, social workers, law enforcement, legislators, and concerned citizens" (66s). In order for communities to benefit from the powerful social control influence of ex-offenders, grassroots programs such as PSI must be supported, rather than inhibited by administrative rules within the prison and legal restrictions on the outside. Keeping transformed offenders incarcerated is wasting their potential to intervene in the lives of criminals who are on the outside. Banning transformed ex-offenders from interactions with other known felons prevents transformed ex-offenders from helping others to become transformed. Strict barriers between transformed ex-offenders on the inside and academics, social workers and citizens on the outside further hinder the expansion of informal social control mechanisms.

Third, public education and awareness of criminal justice research must be improved. Community members need to be aware of research demonstrating that punitive practices and mass incarceration are not effective strategies for giving residents the levels of public safety they desire. The results of criminal-justice related ballot initiatives in California provide a clear example of the lack of public knowledge about criminal justice research. California voters likely voted to approve the construction of more prisons because they believed that this would create safer communities. However, as we have shown, criminological research has found that more prisons do not necessarily translate into safer neighborhoods.

The level of public education and awareness regarding medical or health-related issues provides an illustrative contrast to the low levels of public education regarding criminal justice issues. When scientists within the field of medicine and public health conduct research and come to similar conclusions, these findings are typically transmitted to the public in a timely, clear and meaningful manner. Some elucidatory examples of public knowledge from the health field include the following: Smoking increases your risk of lung cancer. Having unprotected sex increases your risk of sexually transmitted diseases. A poor diet increases your risk of heart disease. These are all facts that have come to be accepted by the public after dissemination from medical researchers and other professionals in the healthcare field. Unfortunately, there is not a similar set of well-known examples from the criminal justice field. Rather, "common knowledge" about crime and justice tends to be dominated by misinformation and oversimplification.[1]

When examining such issues, we have to ask ourselves why criminological research is not communicated in an effective manner, as it is communicated in the public health field. There seem to be several breakdowns in the lines of communication. First, communication between researchers and policymakers / practitioners is quite weak. Policymakers tend to respond to the (often uninformed) demands of the public instead of the social scientific findings of researchers. Second, adequate communication between researchers and the public also seems to be lacking. Major criminological research findings rarely draw the attention of the media, and subsequently, rarely reach the general public.

Strengthening these lines of communication and information sharing between researchers, policymakers, practitioners and the public could improve informal social control through two separate mechanisms. Research can demonstrate to the public the critical role their influence – in the form of informal social control – can play in crime control. Additionally, with a better understanding of the research findings regarding the detrimental effects of mass incarceration, the public will no longer demand an increase in incarceration from policymakers. Returning to the example of California, there is some encouraging movement in this area. While voters unfailingly supported every bond initiative for new prison construction placed on the ballot throughout the 1980s, by the early 1990s, skepticism about the value of this approach grew, and voters stopped so consistently supporting funding for new prison construction initiatives.

Researchers also share some of the burden of more effectively communicating their findings and recommendations to the public. Although criminologists frequently blame the get-tough policy stance favored by politicians on the whims of a vengeful public, public opinion studies do not consistently offer

[1] An example of this type of "common knowledge" about criminal justice is the widely reported "fact" that sex offenders have higher rates of recidivism than other types of offenders. In fact, this

support for this view (e.g., Cullen et al. 2009; King 2008; Applegate, Cullen, and Fisher 1997; Flanagan 1996; McCorkle 1993). No matter what the public opinion research shows, researchers cannot place all the blame for the public's ignorance about research findings on the public alone. Academics and researchers must endeavor to find more effective ways of conveying their messages to the public – in the words of Samuel H. Pillsbury (1995), criminological researchers "must resolve to engage the public, and not just ourselves" (317).

Although at the level of the criminal justice system, altering the complex policy decisions that have resulted in mass incarceration will almost certainly take time (see Auerhahn 2004:113), short-term improvements in informal social control could have important effects on neighborhood crime reduction. By supporting the development and growth of neighborhood associations, the involvement of ex-offenders in informal social control and improving communication between researchers, the public and policymakers, significant improvements in neighborhood crime reduction can be achieved.

Amitai Etzioni cautions that a societal overemphasis on individual rights to the detriment of an emphasis on responsibilities is likely to have the result of restricting individual autonomy, or what he refers to as "oversteering" on the part of governments.[2] Clearly, America's "imprisonment binge" can be characterized as an example of such oversteering. However, he notes that "the more effective the communication lines between those affected and those who do the steering, the less oversteering occurs" (Etzioni 1996:79-80). The realization of the community justice ideal and the fulfillment of the social contract require both that governments be held accountable, *and* that community members (including re-entering offenders) make their voices heard and take an active role in the provision of justice and safety in their communities. It is our hope that the issues raised in this work will help to guide further critical examination of the unintended consequences that result from the operation of the formal justice system from the perspective of community justice, and consideration of the obligations we all assume under the social contract.

---

is patently false – research shows that sex offender recidivism is among the *lowest* for all offense types (see Gaines 2009:16-17).

[2] This assertion is entirely consistent with notions of the relationship between formal and informal social control noted by many scholars, including Rose and Clear (1998), Hunter (1985), Black (1976), and others.

REFERENCES

[1] Allen, F.A. (1981). The decline of the rehabilitative ideal: Penal policy and social purpose. New Haven: Yale University Press.

[2] Applegate, B.K., Cullen, F.T., and Fisher, B.S. (1997). Public support for correctional treatment: The continuing appeal of the rehabilitative ideal. *Prison journal* 77, 237-258.

[3] Auerhahn, K. (2008). Using simulation modeling to evaluate sentencing reform in California: Choosing the future. *Journal of Experimental Criminology*, 4, 241-266.

[4] Auerhahn, K. (2006). Conceptual and methodological issues in the prediction of dangerous behavior. *Criminology and Public Policy*, 5, 801-808.

[5] Auerhahn, K. (2004). California's incarcerated drug offender population, yesterday, today and tomorrow: Evaluating the war on drugs and Proposition 36. *Journal of Drug Issues,* 34, 95-120.

[6] Auerhahn, K. (2003). Selective incapacitation and public policy: Evaluating California's imprisonment crisis. Albany: State University of New York Press.

[7] Auerhahn, K. (2002). "Selective Incapacitation, Three Strikes, and the Problem of Aging Prison Populations." *Criminology and Public Policy*, 1, 353-388.

[8] Auerhahn, K. (1999). Selective incapacitation and the problem of prediction. *Criminology*, 37, 703-733.

[9] Austin, J., Clark, J., Hardyman, P and Henry, D.A. (1999). The impact of 'three strikes and you're out. *Punishment and Society*, 1, 131-162.

[10] Bazemore, G. (1998). The 'community' in community justice: Issues, themes and questions for the new neighborhood sanctioning models." In D.R. Karp (ed.), Community justice: An emerging field (pp. 327-369). New York: Rowman & Littlefield Publishers, Inc.

[11] Bellair, P. (1997). Social interaction and community crime: Examining the importance of neighbor networks. *Criminology*, 35, 677-704.

[12] Black, D. (1976). The behavior of law. San Diego: Academic Press.

[13] Blumstein, A., Cohen, J., and Nagin, D. (eds.). (1978). Deterrence and incapacitation: Estimating the effects of criminal sanctions on crime rates. Washington DC: National Academy of Sciences.

[14] Blumstein, A.and Larson, R. (1969). Models of a total criminal justice system. *Operations Research,* 17, 199-232.

[15] Bridges, G.S. and Crutchfield, R.D. (1988). Law, social standing, and racial disparities in imprisonment. *Social Forces*, 66, 699-724.

[16] Bursik, R. (1988). Social disorganization and theories of crime and delinquency: Problems and prospects. *Criminology,* 26, 519-551.

[17] Bursik, R.J. and Grasmick, H.G. (1993). Neighborhoods and crime: The dimensions of effective community control. New York: Lexington Books.

[18] California Department of Corrections and Rehabilitation. (2008). California out of state correctional facilities. Available online at http://www.cdcr.ca.gov/Visitors/ CA_Out_of_ State_Facilities.html

[19] Canela-Cacho, J.A., Blumstein, A. and Cohen, J. (1997). Relationship between the offending frequency (λ) of imprisoned and free offenders. *Criminology*, 35, 133-175.

[20] Cassidy, R.G. (1985). Modelling a criminal justice system. In D.P. Farrington and R. Tarling (Eds.), *Prediction in criminology* (pp. 193-207). Albany: SUNY Press.

[21] Cassidy, R.G., Peters M.H. and Turner, R.E. (1981). Interrelation of criminal justice system resources and workload. *Infor,* 19, 91-112.

[22] Cassidy, R.G. and Turner, R.E. (1978). Criminal justice system behavior. *Behavioral science,* 23, 99-108.

[23] Chaiken J.M. and Chaiken, M.R. (1982). Varieties of criminal behavior. Santa Monica, CA: Rand.

[24] Clear, T.R. (2007). Imprisoning communities: How mass incarceration makes disadvantaged neighborhoods worse. New York, NY: Oxford University Press.

[25] Clear, T.R. and E. Cadora. (2001). Community Justice. Belmont, CA: Wadsworth Publishing.

[26] Clear, T.R. and Karp, D. R. (1998). "The Community Justice Movement." In D.R. Karp (Ed.), Community justice: An emerging field (pp. 3-28). New York: Rowman & Littlefield Publishers, Inc.

[27] Clear, T.R. and Karp, D.R. (1999). The community justice ideal: Preventing crime and achieving justice. Boulder, CO: Westview Press.

[28] Clear, T.R. and Rose, D.R. (2003). Individual sentencing practices and aggregate social problems. In D.F. Hawkins, S.L. Myers and R. Stone (Eds.), Crime control and social justice: The delicate balance (pp. 27-52). Westport, CT: Greenwood Press.

[29] Clear, T.R., Rose, D.R. and Ryder, J.A. (2001). Incarceration and community: The problem of removing and returning offenders. *Crime and delinquency*, 47, 335-351.

[30] Clear, T.R., Rose, D.R., Waring, E. and Scully, K. (2003). Coercive mobility and crime: A preliminary examination of concentrated incarceration and social disorganization." *Justice quarterly*, 20, 33-64.

[31] Cohen, J. (1983). Incapacitation as a strategy for crime control: Possibilities and pitfalls. In M. Tonry and N. Morris (Eds.), Crime and justice: An annual review of research, volume 5 (pp. 1-84). Chicago: University of Chicago Press.

[32] Cohen, J. (1978). The incapacitative effects of imprisonment: A critical review of the literature. In A. Blumstein, J. Cohen and D. Nagin (Eds.). Deterrence and incapacitation: Estimating the effects of criminal sanctions on crime rates (pp. 187-243). Washington DC: National Academy of Sciences.

[33] Crawford, C., Chiricos, T. and Kleck, G. (1998). Race, racial threat, and sentencing of habitual offenders. *Criminology*, 36, 481-511.

[34] Cullen, F.T., Unnever, J.D., Blevins, K.R., Pealer, J.A., Santana, S.A., Fisher, B.S., and Applegate, B.K. (2009). The myth of public support for capital punishment. In Jane Wood and Theresa Gannon, (Eds.), *Public opinion and criminal justice* (pp. 73-95). Devon, UK: Willan Publishing.

[35] Davis, M. (1995). Hell factories in the field: A prison-industrial complex. The nation, 260, 229-234.

[36] Etzioni, A. (1996). The new golden rule: Community and morality in a democratic society. New York: Basic Books.

[37] Flanagan, T.J. (1996). Reform or punish: Americans' views of the correctional system. In T.J. Flanagan and D.R. Longmire (Eds.), Americans view crime and justice: A national public opinion survey (pp. 75-92). Thousand Oaks, CA: Sage.

[38] Forrester, J.W. (1969). Urban dynamics. Cambridge: MIT Press.

[39] Gaines, J.S. (2009). Labeling adult sex offenders and sexually violent predators: The impact of registration and community notification. Unpublished PhD dissertation, Department of Criminal Justice, Temple University.

[40] Gibson, C., Zhao, J., Lovrich, N. and Gaffney, M. (2002). Social integration, individual perceptions of collective efficacy, and fear of crime in three cities. *Justice quarterly*, 19, 537-564.

[41] Gilbert, M.J. and Settles, T.L. (2007). The next step: Indigenous development of neighborhood-restorative community justice. *Criminal justice review*, 32, 5-25.

[42] Gorton, J. and Boies, J.L. (1999). Sentencing guidelines and racial disparity across time: Pennsylvania prison sentences in 1977, 1983, 1992, and 1993. *Social science quarterly,* 80, 37-54.

[43] Gottfredson, S.D. and Taylor, R.B. (1988). Community contexts and criminal offenders. In T. Hope and M. Shaw (Eds.), Communities and crime reduction (pp. 62-82). London: HMSO.

[44] Greenberg, D. (1975). The incapacitative effect of imprisonment: Some estimates. *Law and society review*, 9, 541-80.

[45] Greenwood, P.W. with Abrahamse, A. (1982). Selective incapacitation. Santa Monica: RAND.

[46] Hanneman, R.A. (1988). Computer-assisted theory building: Modelling dynamic social systems. Beverly Hills, CA: Sage.

[47] Hannon, L. and Knapp, P. (2003). Reassessing nonlinearity in the urban disadvantage / violent crime relationship: An example of methodological bias from log transformation. Criminology, 41, 1427-1448.

[48] Hewitt, J.D. and Clear, T.R. (1983). The impact of sentencing reform: From indeterminate to determinate sentencing. Lanham, MD: University Press of America.

[49] Hughes, T. and Wilson, D. (2009). Reentry trends in the United States. Washington, DC: Bureau of Justice Statistics. Available online at http://www.ojp.usdoj.gov/bjs/reentry/reentry.htm#highlights.

[50] Hunter, A.J. (1985). Private, parochial and public social orders: The problem of crime and incivility in urban communities. In G.D. Suttles and M.N. Zald (Eds.), The challenge of social control: Citizenship and institution building in modern society (pp. 230-242). Norwood, NJ: Aldex Publishing.

[51] Irwin, J. (1985). The jail: Managing the underclass in American society. Berkeley: University of California Press.

[52] Jones, B. (1998). A history of the California initiative process. Sacramento: Secretary of State's Office.

[53] Kadish, S.H. (1978). Introduction. Determinate sentencing: Reform or Regression? Proceedings of the Special Conference on Determinate Sentencing, Boalt Hall School of Law, University of California, Berkeley. Washington, DC: Law Enforcement Assistance Administration, U.S. Department of Justice.

[54] Karp, D.R. (Ed.) (1998). Community justice: An emerging field. Oxford: Rowan & Littlefield.

[55] King, A. (2008). Keeping a safe distance: Individualism and the less punitive public. *British journal of criminology* 48, 190-208.

[56] Kovandzic, T.V. and Vieraitis, L.M. (2006). The effect of county-level prison population growth on crime rates. *Criminology and Public Policy,* 5, 213-244.

[57] Legislative Analyst's Office. (1995). The "three strikes and you're out" law: A preliminary assessment. Available online at http://www.lao.ca.gov/sc010695.html.

[58] Legislative Analyst's Office. (1997). Addressing the state's long-term inmate population growth. Available online at http://www.lao.ca.gov/acrobat_files/pb050297_addressing _ inmate_pop.pdf. Legislative Analyst's Office. (1999). The "three strikes and you're out" law's impact on state prisons: An update. Available online at http://www.lao.ca.gov.

[59] Legislative Analyst's Office. (2005). A primer: Three strikes – the impact after more than a decade. Available online at http://www/lao.ca.gov/3_Strikes/3_strikes102005.htm.

[60] Levitt, S. (1996). The effect of prison population size on crime rates: Evidence from prison overcrowding litigation. The quarterly journal of economics, 111, 319-351.

[61] Liedka, R.V., Piehl, A.M. and Useem, B. (2006). The crime-control effect of incarceration: Does scale matter? *Criminology and public policy*, 5, 245-276.

[62] LIFERS Public Safety Initiative Steering Committee. (2004). Ending the culture of street crime. *Prison journal 84* (supplement), 48s-68s.

[63] Lowenkamp, C.T., Cullen, F.T. and Pratt, T.C. (2003). Replicating Sampson and Groves' test of social disorganization theory: Revisiting a criminological classic. *Journal of research in crime and delinquency,* 40, 351-373.

[64] Lynch, J.P. and Sabol, W.J. (2004a). "Assessing the Effects of Mass Incarceration on Informal Social Control in Communities." *Criminology and Public Policy* 3(2): 267-294.

[65] Lynch, J.P. and Sabol, W.J. (2004b). "Effects of Incarceration on Informal Social Control in Communities." In M. Pattillo, D. Weiman and B. Western (Eds.), Imprisoning America: The social effects of mass incarceration (pp. 135-165). New York: Russell Sage Foundation.

[66] Lynch, J.P., Sabol, W.J., Planty, M. and Shelly, M. (2002). Crime, coercion and community: The effects of arrest and incarceration policies on informal social control in neighborhoods. Washington, D.C.: Urban Institute.

[67] Marvell, T.B. and Moody, C.E. (1994). Prison population growth and crime reduction. *Journal of quantitative criminology*, 10, 109-140.

[68] McCorkle, R.C. (1993). Punish and rehabilitate? Public attitudes toward six common crimes. *Crime and delinquency* 39, 240-252.

[69] Mears, D.P., Wang, X., Hay, C. and Bales, W. D. (2008). Social ecology and recidivism: Implications for prisoner reentry. *Criminology,* 46, 301-340.

[70] Monahan, J. (1978). The prediction of violent criminal behavior: A methodological critique and prospectus. In A. Blumstein, J. Cohen, and D. Nagin (Eds.), Deterrence and incapacitation: Estimating the effects of criminal sanctions on crime rates (pp. 244-269). Washington, DC: National Academy of Sciences.

[71] Monahan, J. (1981). Predicting violent behavior: An assessment of clinical techiniques. Beverly Hills, CA: Sage.

[72] Morenoff, J.D., Sampson, R. and Raudenbush, S.W. (2001). Neighborhood inequality, collective efficacy and the spatial dynamics of urban violence. *Criminology,* 39, 517-560.

[73] Ohlin, L.E. and Remington, F.J. (1993). Discretion in criminal justice: The tension between individualization and uniformity. Albany: SUNY Press.

[74] Petee, T. (1994) Recommended for release on recognizance: Factors affecting pretrial release recommendations. *Journal of social psychology,* 134, 3:375-382.

[75] Pew Center on the States. (2008). One in 100: Behind bars in America 2008. Available online at http://www.pewcenteronthestates.org/uploadedFiles/8015PCTS_Prison08_FINAL_2-1-1_FORWEB.pdf.

[76] Pillsbury, S.H. (1995). Why are we ignored? The peculiar place of experts in the current debate about crime and justice. *Criminal law bulletin* 31, 305-336.

[77] Piquero, A.R., West, V., Fagan, J., and Holland, J. (2006). Neighborhood, race, and the economic consequences of incarceration in New York City, 1985-1996. In R.D. Peterson, L.J. Krivo and J. Hagan (Eds.), The many colors of crime: Inequalities of race, ethnicity and crime in America (pp. 256-273). New York: New York University Press.

[78] Renauer, B.C., Cunningham, W.S., Feyerherm, B., O'Connor, T., and Bellatty, P. (2006). Tipping the scales of justice: The effect of overincarceration on neighborhood violence. *Criminal justice policy review*, 17, 362-379.

[79] Rountree, P. and Kenneth L. (1996). Burglary victimization, perceptions of crime risk, and routine activities: A multilevel analysis across Seattle neighborhoods and census tracts. *Journal of Research in Crime and Delinquency*, 33, 2, 147-180.

[80] Rousseau, Jean-Jacques. (1762 [1968]). The social contract. Maurice Cranston, Trans. New York: Penguin Books.

[81] Rose, D.R. and Clear, T.R. (1998). Incarceration, social capital, and crime: Implications for social disorganization theory. *Criminology*, 36, 441-480.

[82] Sabol, W.J., Minton, T.D. and Harrison, P.M. (2007). Prison and jail inmates at midyear 2006. NCJ 217675. Washington, D.C.: Bureau of Justice Statistics.

[83] Sampson, R.J. (1987). Communities and crime. In M.R. Gottfresdon and T. Hirschi (Eds.), Positive criminology (pp. 91-114). Beverly Hills, CA: Sage.

[84] Sampson, R.J. and Groves, W.B. (1989). Community structure and crime: Testing social disorganization theory. *American journal of sociology*, 94, 774-802.

[85] Sampson, R.J., Raudenbush, S.W. and Earls, F. (1997). Neighborhoods and violent crime: A Multi-level study of collective efficacy. *Science,* 77, 918-924.

[86] Scott, P.D. (1977). Assessing dangerousness in criminals. *British journal of psychiatry*, 131, 124-142.

[87] Shaw, C.R. and McKay, H.D. (1942). Juvenile delinquency in urban areas. Chicago: University of Chicago Press.

[88] Spelman, W. (1994). *Criminal incapacitation.* New York: Plenum.

[89] Spelman, W. (2000). "The limited importance of prison expansion." In A. Blumstein and J. Wallman (Eds.), *The crime drop in America* (pp. 97-129). New York: Cambridge University Press.

[90] Steadman, H.J., and Cocozza, J.J. (1974). Careers of the criminally insane. Lexington, MA: D.C. Heath and Company.

[91] Smith, M. (2001). What future for public safety and restorative justice in a system of community penalties? In A. Bottoms, L. Gelsthorpe and S. Rex (Eds.), Community penalties: Change and challenges (pp. 200-225). Devon, UK: Willan Publishing.

[92] Steury, E.H. and Frank, N. (1990). Gender bias and pretrial release: More pieces of the puzzle. *Journal of criminal justice*, 18, 417-432.

[93] Taylor, R.B. (2001). Breaking away from broken windows: Baltimore neighborhoods and the nationwide fight against crime, grime, fear and decline. New York: Westview.

[94] Taylor, R.B. (2002). Fear of crime, local social ties, and collective efficacy: Maybe masquerading measurement, maybe déjà vu all over again. *Justice quarterly*, 19, 773-792.

[95] Thornberry, T.P. and Jacoby, J.E. (1979). The criminally insane: A community follow-up of mentally ill offenders. Chicago: University of Chicago Press.

[96] Tonry, M. (1995). Malign neglect: Race, crime, and punishment in America. New York: Oxford University Press.

[97] Turner, S. (1999). Profiling inmates in the Los Angeles County jail: Risks, recidivism, and release options. Paper Presented at National Institute of Justice Annual Conference on Criminal Justice Research and Evaluation, July 18-21, 1999, Washington, DC.

[98] Veysey, B.M. and Messner, S.F. (1999). Further testing of social disorganization theory: An elaboration of Sampson and Groves' 'community structure and crime.' *Journal of research in crime and delinquency*, 36, 156-174.

[99] Walker, N. (1991). Why punish? Theories of punishment reassessed. Oxford: Oxford University Press.

[100] Wildavsky, A. (1979). Speaking truth to power: The art and craft of policy analysis. New Brunswick: Transaction Publishers.

[101] Wilson, W.J. (1987). The truly disadvantaged: The inner city, the underclass and public policy. Chicago: University of Chicago Press.

[102] Wooldredge, J. (2002). Examining the (Ir)relevance of aggregation bias for multilevel studies of neighborhoods and crime with an example comparing census tracts to official neighborhoods in Cincinnatti. *Criminology,* 40, 3, 681-709.

[103] Zimbardo, P.G. (1994). Transforming California's prisons into expensive old age homes for felons: Enormous hidden costs for California's taxpayer. San Francisco: Center on Juvenile and Criminal Justice.

[104] Zimring, F.E. and Hawkins, G. (1995). Incapacitation: Penal confinement and the restraint of crime. New York: Oxford University Press.

[105] Zimring, F.E., Hawkins, G., and Kamin, S. (2001). Punishment and democracy: Three strikes and you're out in California. New York: Oxford University Press.

INDEX

A

B

C

D

E

F

G

H

I

J

K

L

M

N

O

P

Q

R

S

T

U

V

W